THE PROBLEM OF METAPHYSICS

THE PROBLEM OF
METAPHYSICS

D. M. MACKINNON

*Norris-Hulse Professor of Divinity
in the University of Cambridge*

CAMBRIDGE UNIVERSITY PRESS

Published by the Syndics of the Cambridge University Press
Bentley House, 200 Euston Road, London NW1 2DB
American Branch: 32 East 57th Street, New York, N.Y. 10022

© Cambridge University Press 1974

Library of Congress Catalogue Card Number: 73–79309

ISBN: 0 521 20275 2

First published in 1974

Printed in Great Britain by
Western Printing Services Ltd
Bristol

Contents

Preface

This book contains the substance of the Gifford Lectures delivered under the same title before the University of Edinburgh in the springs of 1965 and 1966. The material has, however, been drastically revised, sometimes shortened and sometimes expanded. The resulting work is hardly worthy of the illustrious foundation under whose auspices the Lectures were delivered; but it represents an attempt to discuss certain fundamental questions relating to the nature and possibility of metaphysics, and is offered as a contribution to a discussion that is likely to continue for a very long time.

It would be impossible for me to list the many individuals and institutions of learning to whom I am indebted in the preparation of this book, but I must offer my most sincere thanks to the University of Edinburgh for the invitation received in January 1964 to prepare and deliver the Gifford Lectures for the next two years, for the great honour done to me by this invitation and for the many kindnesses extended to my wife and myself during the periods we spent in Edinburgh in 1965 and 1966. I should like also in this connection to mention both the Principal of the University and Lady Swann, and the staff of the various departments, philosophical and theological, both for the help they gave in the presentation of the Lectures and for giving me the opportunity to discuss them after they were delivered with members of the audience.

But my greatest debt is to my wife, both for her ceaseless patience and goodness to me during the preparation of the Lectures and still more of the book in which their substance is presented; and also for the very many suggestions she made and references to which she called my attention in the worlds of poetry and art, in which she is always a teacher and I myself never more than a learner.

D. M. MacKinnon

Cambridge, 1972

vii

1

Introduction

To introduce the central theme of this book, I propose to offer a very brief sketch of two conceptions of descriptive metaphysics (to borrow the very useful phrase of Professor P. F. Strawson). These conceptions are those of Aristotle and Kant, and with them we shall in different ways be occupied throughout the whole work; this though much more explicit attention will be paid to Kant's ideas than Aristotle's. Yet the latter will continually make their influence felt throughout the argument. For very different though their concerns and methods were, Aristotle and Kant can be bracketed together as practitioners of descriptive metaphysics in that while both of them have very definite *Weltanschauungen*, they both carried out systematic enquiries aimed at laying bare the most fundamental and pervasive features of the world around us, the manner in which those features are interrelated and the identity and nature of those concepts revealed by analysis to be involved in all descriptive and referential discourse. Inevitably there must be oversimplification and specialists either in Kantian or in Aristotelian studies will no doubt find much in this outline to outrage their scholarly sensibilities; but it may be that the outlines offered will enable the experts to return again to the field of their special knowledge and see things which neither I, nor they, had noticed before.

It would be maintained, almost without question, that Kant, in the first half of the *Critique of Pure Reason*, was both trying to give as satisfactory an account as he could of our ultimate conceptual scheme, and at the same time, and as part of the same enquiry, to give an inventory of the fundamental *structural* features of the world in which we find ourselves. Moreover, he was concerned to show, where the structural features of our world were concerned, that these features, and these features only, *must* be exemplified in any objective world with which we might suppose ourselves concerned.

1

Kant's descriptive metaphysics

1. Kant in the *Critique of Pure Reason* is determined to reveal (as he believes completely and exhaustively) the ways in which conceptual thinking is diversified. Such thinking he regards as fundamentally an activity of recognition, in which we identify particulars as being of certain sorts (e.g. a given animal as a tabby-cat) or certain relatively restricted sorts, as belonging to more general sorts (e.g. anything with the properties of a tabby-cat as belonging to the feline species). He may indeed be claimed as anticipating to some extent the treatment of concepts as recognitional capacities by modern philosophers. This we may illustrate by a quite sophisticated legal example. If one asks a man whether he has a clear concept of 'contempt of court', we are asking him whether he can recognise the presence of 'contempt' in certain kinds of public discussion of matters *sub judice* as well as in the behaviour of a witness who arrives in court to give evidence indisputably under the influence of alcoholic drink.

Kant's 'pure categories' are second order concepts, concepts of ways in which these recognitional capacities are exercised. If we say that the category of ground and consequent is 'a pure concept of the understanding', we are not suggesting that it is a recognitional capacity of an exceptional degree of refinement and resulting width of application (as e.g. the conception of gravitational force), but that it is the conception of the way in which in exercise of our understanding, we entertain the relevance of determining what is the case in respect of one state of affairs to determining what is the case in respect of another. This form of understanding is in play in the most diverse enquiries. Thus, we encounter it in a *reductio ad absurdum* proof in mathematics, and again in such historical judgements (expressed in terms of a counter factual conditional) as 'If Hannibal had marched on Rome after the battle of Cannae, he would have taken the city.' In this last case the answer to the question whether he marched on the city after the battle is presented as relevant to the answer to the question whether or not he took it.

2. But this enquiry, to which the section of the *Critique of Pure Reason* known as the 'Metaphysical Deduction of the Categories' is devoted (and to which Kant returns in his third and last critique, the *Critique of Judgement*), is introduced in the argument of his first critique as the essential first stage in a distinguishable enquiry, namely his enquiry concerning the structural features of the world

in which we find ourselves, with which we have commerce through senses, and by contrast with which indeed, in its unyielding public order, we come to recognise our own private, personal autobiography. We suppose that in all our experience we have to do with a world belonging to a single space, enduring through a single time, in which there are relatively permanent, identifiable things which provide us with reference points for the marking of environmental changes, whose constancy is as much a matter of natural law as the occurrence of the observed changes which we note and plot in their relations one with another with ever-increasing sophistication. It is with such matters as these that Kant is concerned in such sections of the *Critique of Pure Reason* as the 'Aesthetic', the 'Transcendental Deduction' and the 'Analogies of Experience'. Certainly, there are here certain very important differences of emphasis between stretches of his argument that must be noted, differences which are not confined to apparent contradictions between the first edition of the 'Deduction' of 1781 and the second of 1787.

(a) Thus, at times, Kant seems concerned chiefly to develop an extremely subtle and deeply suggestive account of the constant condition of human perceptual experience, and in particular of the role in such experience of self-awareness, imaging, imagination, memory and conceptual thought. In the course of this enquiry he probes the difference between the sort of self-consciousness to which an individual may win his way through grasping the particular factors that have co-operated to give his personal biography the shape it has assumed, and the kind of self-awareness (called by Kant 'pure apperception') that accompanies as its formal subjective condition the very possibility of any sort of awareness of the world to which we belong as a continuous whole and any sort of questioning concerning that world and our own place in its history.

It may be that the point can be grasped by us by an example Kant does not himself employ, namely the plight of the amnesiac. Such a man knows that he has in fact a past and that to this past there belongs not only the secret of his personal identity but the causes of his being where he now is, e.g. in a hospital ward in a town with which he can recall no sort of association. Yet, in this instance he is only able to pose his problem to himself and to understand it when put to him by others because he knows what a town is, what it is to be in a hospital, etc. If we suppose a case in which the amnesiac is unable to identify a hospital ward, doctors, nurses, etc., for what they are, seeming indeed ignorant even of the sense of the word 'town', we find ourselves moving towards a very different sort of situation, and one which we find it very hard, if not impossible, to conceive. We certainly find it difficult to conceive the plight of an amnesiac whose ability to frame to himself his own problem is jeopardised by loss of all sense of a past, of an order of events at once independent of himself and yet as involving him, of a place in the same space as he now is from which he came to the bed in which he lies, etc. We are familiar with conditions in which we say of a man in a prolonged coma after a motor accident that such a man has become a 'living vegetable'. Yet, such language is used to indicate the sort of breakdown of communication which must follow the disintegration of all sense of the structural constants of our world. The amnesiac does not know who he is: yet he knows he has an identity and in this knowledge he is preserved by his capacity to reach *in principle* beyond the present to integrate in a coherent order the *disjecta membra* of his history and experience.

It is characteristic of Kant's extraordinary philosophical power that at the same time as he submits to very searching criticism Hume's account of self-identity, he avoids the mistake of ignoring Hume's sharp judgement on Descartes' unsophisticated supposition of a substantial spiritual self as something immediately intuited. The subjectivity which he regards as ultimate and irreducible is formal, something that can only be grasped when presented as the ultimate subjective condition of a unitary experience from which it *cannot* be prised apart and regarded as some sort of ontologically indestructible element in the world. Kant's advances on Hume in fundamental questions in the philosophy of psychology provide the foundations of his relentless criticism (in the 'Paralogisms of Rational Psychology') of traditional metaphysical argument for the immortality of the soul which finds its alleged point of departure in a failure to grasp the limited and relative character of the irreducible uniqueness of status we have to concede to the unitary subject in experience.

(b) Yet, Kant combines this intense concentration on the subjective aspects of human experience with a differently orientated attempt to vindicate our conviction that in the world of which we have commerce through the senses, there are *of necessity* certain structural constraints. Thus, it is a world in which we have to reckon with things to which events happen and, moreover, do not happen at random but in accordance with laws. Thus, a sudden drastic change in our environment, an explosion or an earthquake, both alike quite unforeseen, is something whose antecedents we seek,

4

confident that in time we shall find the necessary sufficient conditions of its occurrence. We may, indeed, be totally mistaken in our first identification of the cause, whether made tentatively or confidently. Similarly, where those features of our environment are concerned which we treat as the things to which events happen, or (an element in the traditional conception of substance) as the constant self-contained wholes seemingly quite unaffected by the sorts of changes to which we ourselves and our more immediate environment are subject, we may wilfully ignore the extent to which their very constancy is itself in part determined by inclusive environmental processes by which we ourselves are affected. Thus, we say that 'the rocks remain', acknowledging the slowness of their weathering and contrasting their recognisable immunity to violent upheaval with the vulnerability of the world both of natural objects and of artefacts which we know to be less resistant to storm, to erosion, etc.

In lectures given in the hall of Trinity College, Oxford, in the Hilary Term, 1934, on the conceptions of substance and causality with special reference to the philosophies of Hume and Kant (to which I owe an abiding debt), Professor H. H. Price (who was indeed not yet a professor at the time) emphasised what he called the 'although' character discernible in the working out of natural laws. Once (to use a modern phrase) a chain-reaction had been set in motion or a process begun (e.g. the detonation of an explosive, a drastic movement in a geological fault), granted that the initial stages of the process are the necessary and sufficient conditions of its outcome, apart from effective interference, whether natural or contrived, that outcome will follow. Although one might have it otherwise, these are the ways in which such changes take place. Further, there are in the world a very large number of processes of change quite independent one of another. Thus, the rapid inflow of the tide floods the beach in complete independence of the bodily metabolic changes, or alternating psychological moods, of strollers who walk along the shore at the time. It is a romantic cliché to speak of the 'indifference' of such movement to human feeling. Similarly, a man may indulge in anthropomorphic invocation of the hills in front of him: 'What changes have these great hills seen across the centuries?' Hills do not see either as man or as cats undoubtedly see. Moreover, their surface has been weathered across the centuries and many disturbances of one sort or another have altered their contours, sometimes suddenly rendering their appearance quite unfamiliar to the surprised climber approaching a route that he thought he knew, to find the rock surface so altered that his projected climb has to be abandoned. Again, the first emergence of these hills remains a datable event in that same time-order to which the speaker's reverie belongs; they were not always there (whatever the force of 'there' in that expression). Yet, their gradual changes are changes within a total *Gestalt* that is relatively self-contained and both the endurance of that *Gestalt* and the *relative* insignificance of the changes in question are recognised as causally independent of the chains of events that take their course under their shadow. Certainly this self-containedness is an instance of the working of natural law; a man makes himself foolish who shakes his fist in the face of the hills as if he momentarily thought his anger substitute for the faith of which it was said that it could move mountains! Yet, if we discern the working of natural law in the constancy of the hills, we must not suppose that the writ of causal explanation runs any less in respect of the courses of events of which we have spoken as taking place within their shadow. Such courses follow their own routes, independent of the hills, independent also very often one of another. Of course, the routes may intersect, furnishing the imaginative writer or even some less sophisticated commentator with instances of what he must call coincidence.

It is with such features of the world of our experience as I have illustrated and the justification with which we assume their constant presence as necessary, indispensable conditions of objectively referential statement that Kant is concerned in his first *Critique*. But all the time, when the emphasis falls in his argument where I have now placed it, invoking a large number of examples to compensate the extreme abstract character of his exposition, Kant seeks to rejoin in the end the emphasis of 2 (a) by suggesting that treatment of what is presented to us by the senses as disclosure of a fragment of such a world is necessary to our including it within a total experience ascribable to a single subject.

3. Further, Kant well knew as his *Inaugural Dissertation* of 1770 effectively illustrates, that the notions of substance, causality, unity, existence, possibility, necessity, were fundamental tools of traditional transcendent metaphysical speculation. In the *Dissertation*, Kant developed his own account of the proper method of metaphysical speculation and a considerable part of the *Critique of Pure Reason* is devoted to exposing the mistakes that he had become convinced he had there made. We are entitled to treat the concepts

of substance and causality as concepts of fundamental, uniquely pervasive, necessarily permanent features of the world around us. Yet, we are not entitled to use them in an attempt to estimate the relations of the conditioned to the unconditioned, the relative to the absolute. We have to reckon with the fact that human beings are impelled by the exigencies of their intellectual natures to aspire to the ultimate and unconditioned. There is indeed something of profound positive significance in such aspiration; but if men are not to be betrayed by it into sterile, futile or destructive disputation, it must be disciplined, and the road to the successful achievement of such discipline lay by way of the sort of conceptual analysis, indeed appraisal, of conceptual thinking as such, to which the *Critique of Pure Reason* is devoted.

4. While Kant emphasises the spontaneity of understanding, and of that imagination which in one place he characterises as the 'understanding working blind', it is fundamental to his whole argument that neither understanding nor imagination creates its own objects. For Kant, to come to know what is the case is a finding, not a fashioning. Yet the ways of finding out, although it is Kant's claim that they express an underlying unity, have their own internal complexity, and (as I have said) the detail of their operation, *in concreto*, evokes from him some of his most painstaking and searching work in the philosophy of perception. For all this he never abandons his underlying loyalty to the common-sense conviction that in coming to know we do not construct a world of our own fashioning, but compel that which is given to us to yield its secrets in ways admitting of our assimilation.

To this point he returns in a very illuminating passage towards the end of his third *Critique* – the *Critique of Judgement*, where he contrasts human with divine understanding, what he calls the *intellectus ectypus* with the *intellectus archetypus*. He is, in this passage, in no sense arguing for or against the existence of God; rather, he is helping his readers to attain a firmer purchase-hold on the limits of their characteristically intellectual activity. If God exists, then what he knows he himself creates, and therefore what he knows is immediately transparent to him. In the *Critique of Judgement*, what Kant is chiefly concerned to bring out is that God (again if he exists) does not have to argue inductively, to carry out experiments, to revise conceptions in the light of further observation; whereas we need to do all these things. Yet Kant is also making, in this passage, the much more general point that our understanding does not create its own objects; this we come to grasp when we contrast our understanding with an understanding that *does* create its own objects.

Concepts for Kant are (as I said at the outset) basically capacities of recognition, and our ultimate conceptual scheme is the manner in which these capacities are diversified in their operation. So, with the notion of existence, to take a familiar example, we ask whether the Loch Ness Monster exists, or whether there is a Loch Ness Monster. In asking the question we assume that the state of affairs about which we are enquiring is possible, even though, of course, we may not be clear precisely what sort of entity would have to be found in Loch Ness to satisfy the description 'the Loch Ness Monster'. Unexpected questions calling for conceptual decision may arise, although we may be sure from the outset that we would not affirm the monster to be there, if we discovered a floating log of unusual size and shape, assuming in certain lights, especially in the eyes of persons returning from places of public refreshment, the likeness of a large moving creature! If we end by answering in the affirmative the question whether the monster exists, we emerge from a state of ignorance, advancing beyond the admission of bare possibility to one of the affirmation of existence. Yet we do not find any necessity in this existence comparable to that which we have to acknowledge in a logical demonstration, or in the operation of a natural law. The distinction between existence, possibility, and necessity, with which Kant is concerned in his discussion of the categories of modality, is a distinction whose whole significance only becomes plain when it is recognised as a distinction drawn in terms of the modes of operation of such an understanding as we find ours to be. Of course, Kant's philosophy of logic is extremely crude and unsophisticated by the standards of modern modal logic; but what he is saying is clear enough, and the principles of his treatment have emerged from my discussion. Yet, I have said this study of the forms of our understanding is integrated with his attempt in the 'Transcendental Deduction of the Categories' to establish the limits of that experience, the features that must be manifested by any world of which we are to make intelligible assertions. Thus we insist, and for Kant we are right to insist, that whatever matter of fact we refer to must fall within an all-embracing single space and time. What, for instance, a radio-astronomer asserts concerning events $3\frac{1}{2}$ thousand million light years away must[1] belong to the same time-order as the writing

---

[1] The relation of this 'must' to the 'must' of entailment and to that of a law of nature is a central problem in the interpretation of Kant's *First Critique*.

of this chapter, the last football match between Rangers and Celtic to be played in Glasgow, and the forthcoming examinations in the University of Cambridge. Kant believes (as I have said) that he can prove that there are certain features which must belong to anything whatsoever concerning which we make intelligible assertion; whatever we say must be capable of statement in terms of what is qualitatively similar to what we experience, if it is to be regarded as endowed with objective import. Moreover, the characteristics which mark out this qualitative similarity can and must be plotted. The choice, as an example here, of the single space and time which Kant so stresses is deliberate, for I should like to register an underlying hostility to the view some-times put forward (as if it were a sort of revelation) that the time-order in which historical events occur is somehow quite different from the order in which natural events occur. It is part of Kant's achievement to have drawn attention to the continuities of natural and historical existence, of which the more obviously historical natural sciences (for instance, geology) should make us immediately aware. Yet notoriously for Kant genetically space and time were subjective forms of outer and inner sense.

5. So, in conclusion of this part of my study, I must emphasise Kant's anthropocentrism. It is indeed to bring out this fundamental aspect of his thinking that I introduced a reference to the passage in the *Critique of Judgement* as well as the reminder of his treatment of space and time as objective forms of sensibility. Our point of view as experients is the human point of view, our world a world marked by the conditions under which alone experience is possible for us. And indeed, at this point it is fitting that I should indicate my realisation that extended treatment of Kant's philosophy must involve deep appraisal of the role in his theory of knowledge of synthesis. Certainly, reflection on the use he makes of this notion emphasises his sense of the relativity of the human point of view, especially when the implications of carefully drawn distinction between intuitive and discursive understandings are drawn. At the deepest level for Kant to prove the indispensability for objective human experience of such categories as substance and causality is to lay hold on the inherently limited character of the experience which they make possible, and indeed to suggest immediately that if Kant is to develop any philosophical theology, that theology must fall within the tradition of negative theology.

Aristotle's descriptive metaphysics
We pass now to Aristotle. Professor Knowles has brilliantly characterised Aristotle as foremost 'amongst those who have sought to
trace the veins and sinews of substance'.[2] But how are we to understand this exploration?

It is very easy to accuse Aristotle, as the late Professor R. G.
Collingwood did in his *Essay on Metaphysics*,[3] of finding the subject-
matter of 'first philosophy' in the most general of all abstract concepts, namely that of being, and to follow him in stigmatising this
subject-matter as vacuous, and its study as sterile. Yet to treat being
as a *summum genus* is to ignore the doctrine, both of the *Metaphysics*
and of the *Categories* alike. In the sixth chapter of the first book of
the *Nicomachean Ethics*, Aristotle insists that the categories are a
developing series; in *Metaphysics*, Γ II, he amplifies this doctrine,
seeming to oscillate between defining the subject-matter of metaphysics as substance, and as being. Yet there are modes of being that
are manifestly non-substantial. When we predicate in the category
of accident, when, for instance, we affirm Socrates to be snub-nosed,
we certainly take for granted that being snub-nosed is a mode of
being. But being snub-nosed is not being a substance or thing. Yet
it is arguable that if there were no things as men, there would be
nothing to be snub-nosed. If we predicate his manhood of Socrates,
we predicate what is the condition both of his being snub-nosed and
of his being a philosopher. Again, he might have philosophised without being snub-nosed and been snub-nosed without philosophising. Of
course we know well that a man's physical appearance may affect
deeply his life and behaviour. A grotesque may seek compensation in
intellectual activity. We are on edge in the presence of Aristotle's
repeated loyalty to a conception of individuality (arguably at war
were his deepest insights over substance) that finds the principle of
individuation in spatially locatable matter.

Yet, however deficient we may find this tendency in Aristotle's
thought to invest the universal with greater dignity than the particular, even while insisting against Plato on the ontological primacy of
the concrete thing, we have to allow that his categories of being form
a developing series to the extent that, for instance, a philosopher's
manhood is presupposed by his philosophising, that his being in a
particular place at a particular time, although possibly significant

[2] *The Evolution of Mediaeval Thought* (Longmans, 1962).
[3] (O.U.P., 1940), pp. 3–20.

for his development as an individual, may touch him less intimately as a human being than his intellectual commitment, that only a man who has seen can become blind, etc. There is good sense in insisting that some at least of the relations into which a thing, whether natural or artefact, enters with other things leave quite unaffected what the thing in question is in itself. Thus, one pencil remains what it is whether it be laid to the left or to the right of another, and its character as a pencil is unaffected by a writer's choice of it rather than its neighbour to make notes for a book that he is writing. Of course, the result of his choice will be its wearing out more quickly than its neighbour; but in the moment of choice it is one pencil beside another and as such it is chosen. It is such considerations as these that led Aristotle to treat substance as the most fundamental form of being, to which all other forms were relative one way or another.

The lines of thought indicated by the examples given do combine to suggest that substance is in important respects fundamental to quality, accident, relation, deprivation, etc., but that in this peculiar relativity these forms retain their peculiar dignity.

Aristotle finds an analogy to this sort of priority in the relation of the health we predicate of human bodies to that which we predicate, for instance, of a diet or of a watering place. It is not that when we predicate health in the latter cases we are affirming something *unconditionally* relative to the extent to which observation of the one, or residence in the other, actually advances the health of careful followers of the prescribed régime, or of visitors to the watering place mentioned. Yet the bodily organism is the field of the 'nuclear' realisation of health,[4] even as for Kant in the *Grundlegung* the individual's realisation of a particular policy of life, embodied in his choices and affirmed in the principles whereby he disciplines his motives, is the sun of the universe of value. Alone of all excellences such realisation is without shadow of ambivalence of the kind which may infect good health,[5] high intelligence, let alone financial independence and a capacity to use it to one's best advantage. There is a fascinating correspondence between Kant's scheme of value as in a peculiar sense relative to its supposed 'nuclear' realisation in moral excellence, and Aristotle's treatment of forms of being as polarised on substance. Indeed, towards the end of his detailed

---

[4] Blackpool remains healthy, if after a visit there, one needs a time in a clinic before returning to work.
[5] 'Health' finds here its focal meaning.

analysis of the predication of good, in the sixth chapter of the first book of the *Nicomachean Ethics*, Aristotle does briefly suggest himself that goods may be one, as being is, through an orientation towards, or derivation from, a fundamental realisation.

Yet to return to the topic of substance, for Aristotle that which is substantial is that which *is* fundamentally. The whole pattern of our conceptual organisation is pivoted on that which exists of itself. It is noteworthy that Aristotle even treats *steresis* or deprivation as a mode of being. Only that which is may be deprived; only the seeing (actually or potentially) can suffer blindness. Yet he is doing more than simply deploy the fundamental patterns of conceptual organisation, offering a comprehensive account of the detailed interrelation of those notions we find ourselves using in discourse concerning every sort of subject-matter, such notions as thing and property, existence, truth, etc. These notions are indeed so pervasive that if, in certain fields, we are betrayed by their injudicious employment to seek substances corresponding to the substantives we use, and have to discipline ourselves against this fallacy, we are betrayed in this way just because the notion is indeed so fundamental that we are easily tricked into supposing it present when it is out of place. For instance, it is tempting to treat expressions designating nation-states etc. as referring to substantial entities. What we say concerning them simulates what we say when we speak of the properties of things, and their relations to other things. Yet it is surely quite clear that nation-states are not substances, and that it is a dangerous mistake to suppose them to be so. In such cases we have to be on guard because it is only too easy to suppose what is fundamental in description and referential discourse to be in play when, for instance, we speak of one nation declaring war upon another.

Certainly Aristotle is attempting an account of our most fundamental concepts;[6] but he is doing more than that. In some sense he is saying what the fundamental sorts of thing in the world are. It is indeed his commitment to this enterprise that justifies to some small extent Collingwood's charge that he regards metaphysics as the supremely comprehensive investigation, because it is concerned with that which is most abstractly universal. True, Collingwood is wrong in failing to recognise that for Aristotle being is not a generic universal, but a transcendental one which manifests a peculiar sort of analogical unity. Yet that which manifests such a unity Aristotle identified in the end with the most fundamental sorts of thing there

[6] His understanding of the concept is significantly different from Kant's.

are in the world, in the peculiar dependence of lower form upon higher. When we turn to the world whose characteristic processes he sets out in such varied treatises as the *Physics*, the *de Partibus Animalium*, and the *de Generatione et Corruptione*, we find that what there is satisfies in its fundamental forms, the conditions of his categories. It is often suggested that his treatise on the soul, *de Anima*, is to be understood as a biological treatise; but if one simply mentions one of its most characteristic doctrines, namely that the soul is the form of the body, this most important and obscure doctrine remains unintelligible unless we take for granted that in the world there are substances. Moreover, we are at once reminded of the central crux of the exploration of substance in the *Metaphysics*, namely whether substance is to be identified with form, or with the concrete compact of the union of form and matter, and again whether form is universal or particular. Yet when Aristotle comes to discuss what it is to be a human being, it is the pattern of being polarised upon substance which is in play.

For Aristotle the proposition that there are substances is a true existential proposition. Certainly he is tantalisingly and most suggestively contradictory in his answer to the question whether these substances should be identified with concrete individuals ('composites of matter and form'), or with that which makes them what they are. Here indeed is the central crux, less of his system than of his exploration. Yet in learning that there are substances, we learn what all things in the world are fundamentally like.

It is Aristotle's view that truth resides in the correspondence of thought and things. A doctrine of categories is therefore, before all else for him, an account of the ways in which things are. The metaphysician, to give the practitioner of first philosophy his traditional name, is concerned to explore that to which the statements we make ultimately refer. I say explore; perhaps I had better said that the metaphysician seeks to lay bare the anatomical structure of what it is that in the end we are referring to. Certainly Aristotle's own practice shows that the metaphysician will require a real capacity for penetrating behind the smoke-screens set up by the ways in which we represent to ourselves what it is we refer to. Thus we say that when we speak truly we are referring to that which is, but what is it for a thing to be? Men and women, tables and chairs, thunderstorms and earthquakes, discoveries and acts of self-sacrifice, virtues and vices, shapes and sizes, truth and false judgement – all these in some sense are. But if we suppose that when we say they *are*, we speak univocally, as if they *were* in exactly the same way, we are in danger of obscuring from ourselves the ways in which these very different modes of being are related one to the other. We know that there are very important differences between, for instance, a man and a thunderstorm, a generous disposition and an act of self-sacrifice, an opportunity and a deprivation. Aristotle's enquiries had themselves been deeply affected by his conviction that the sort of criticisms Plato had himself brought against his own theory of forms in the *Parmenides* were soundly based; indeed, he implies that in his later dialogues Plato had gone some way towards extricating from the context of that speculative metaphysical theory the insights it actually contained concerning the ways in which things are. In other words, Aristotle saw himself as perfecting the safe deliverance of a genuine descriptive metaphysics from the highly revisionary enterprise in which, in Plato's work, it had first seen the light. Yet for him a descriptive metaphysics was something more than the mere articulation of fundamental conceptual structure; it gave us information of a kind at once extremely elusive and extremely familiar, concerning the world about us. Yet, of course, as we will know, Aristotle's metaphysical enterprise was not confined to the analytical task of fundamental description; he had his own extremely interesting, if highly obscure, speculative vision, cosmological in structure, but invoking ideas developed in his conceptual analyses in its articulation.

The account given of Aristotle is much briefer than that of Kant and is open to criticism for its failure to treat at any length the remarkable contradictions that beset Aristotle's explorations, let alone the development and elaboration of his ideas by the mediaeval schoolmen and their exhaustive concern with such questions as the relations of essence and existence. Much of Aristotle's analytical work in the *Metaphysics* would be said by many to belong to the field of the philosophy of logic and to have its place alongside, e.g. Frege's defence of the view that cardinal numbers are objects, part of the furniture of the world, and his inevitable consequent engagement with the general question, what sorts of thing qualify to be regarded as objects and therefore as part of their furniture.

Further, though there is a gulf between Aristotle's ontological analysis and his cosmological theology and one may learn from the latter and reject the former, the gulf is not one conceived as Kant conceived it almost in the tradition of negative theology. In Kant we are aware of the sort of emphasis into which Plato is constrained, when in the first section of the *Parmenides* he explores the relation of particulars to forms, whereas for Aristotle the cure for such malaise is at hand in more effective analysis of the notions of change and motion, and more particularly of that which changes. Plato and Kant are often practitioners of negative theology, linked also by a prevailing moral concern, whereas Aristotle combines a greater confidence in the continuity of ontological analysis and cosmological exposition.

When the schoolmen invoked Aristotle's doctrine of the 'Analogy of Being', quickly recognising the theological potentialities both of his way of conceiving the unity of the categories by reference to substance and of his sensitivity to the kind of conceptual unity he illustrates by his treatment of *having* in the last chapter of the *Categories*,[7] they invoked this doctrine to attempt to resolve problems more clearly stated in the Platonic tradition. If they found in analogy a middle way between univocity and equivocity (between the unity of generic and specific identity, and that of chance homonymity), they welcomed this middle way as one between the crude over-confidence of the anthropomorphist and the aphasia of the agnostic. From Plato as well as from the prophets of the Old Testament scriptures they had learnt to regard the anthropomorphist's aberration the greater intellectual offence (the intellectual counterpart of the sin of idolatry). In speaking of God the negative way leading towards *aphasia* must be followed before that of eminence; so disciplined the latter might become a way on which analogical predication and comparison as understood by Aristotle might be practised. It was not simply the Christian doctrine of creation that gave a new slant to their enquiries, but a kind of sensitivity to the problems of negative theology, which enabled them to quarry in the body of Aristotle's work for a method, whereby they could avoid the choice between anthropomorphism and aphasia.

Aristotle was no anthropomorphist; his account of the divine activity in *Metaphysics* Λ proves this.[8] But his *Weltanschauung* enabled him to find in substance the notion by which he could bring into relation cosmologically the temporal and the eternal. It was partly the strongly empirical criticism of elements in his Platonic inheritance that enabled him to do this – but the student of his metaphysics is left with the uneasy sense that it was only when the

[7] See appended note.
[8] See the valuable treatment of this matter in Professors G. E. M. Anscombe and Peter Geach, *Three Philosophers* (Blackwell, 1962).

schoolmen infused Platonic agnostic emphasis into their reception of their Aristotelian inheritance that a supreme effort was made to indicate the great gulf fixed between finite and infinite substance and the sort of qualification that must beset *any attempt even to characterise* that gulf as *a gulf*. It is in Kant's philosophical work, with its simultaneous Platonic and Aristotelian resonances, that these issues are most sharply raised for the contemporary student of the problem of metaphysics.

Appended Note: Analogy illustrated by Aristotle's treatment of having in the Categories

In this chapter Aristotle asks what various forms of *having* have in common. A man has a wife entails that he is married to a woman. If however he has a large sum of money at his disposal, this does not entail that he is married to his bank balance. Again a man may have some valuable antiques; but if he treats his wife as if she belonged together with them, he is in for trouble. Similarly a man may have a hole in his trouser pocket; he would not call this a possession. Yet in saying that he has such a hole, it says something about his present state; but when we say that he has a bad temper, we do not imply that he is presently raging; we refer to something about him distinguishable from his married state, and his profession. Again we say that all cases of 'black measles' have certain features in common; we do not suggest here anything akin to possession, rather the exemplification of certain universals (for Aristotle necessarily *in rebus*). Yet these very different forms of having are not classed as such because they are chance homonyms (as e.g. a papal Bull and a prize-winning Aberdeen Angus bull): nor arguably is it simply a matter of metaphor in as much as there is some sort of community present.

2

'Thrusting against the limits of language': an aspect of Plato's *Republic*

This chapter and the next are linked closely together, and serve to crystallise the central topics of this work: what it is to be 'metaphysically minded', how being 'metaphysically minded' involves a 'thrusting against the limits of language', and what claims, if any, can be made for the truth or falsity of the yield of such thrusts? Inevitably at this stage I have to select and so reveal the bias of my own interest and the kind of revisionary or speculative metaphysics to which I am myself drawn.

In a recently published fragment of Wittgenstein's on ethics[1] that philosopher uses the same metaphor, or quasi-metaphor, as the one from which I have derived the title of this chapter. For him, being metaphysically minded (in the way in which the man who is deeply puzzled concerning the foundations of morality may be said to be so) involves a continual thrust or pressure against the familiar confines of intelligible descriptive discourse. The imagery is, of course, that of a man in prison, and intelligible discourse is presented in the rather high-flown guise of a wall or barrier that confines and hems him in. The image may quite properly be criticised as biased in its suggestion, and as indifferent to the kind of freedom men undoubtedly enjoy when they have mastered the limits of such discourse. Yet Wittgenstein's language effectively brings out the extent to which the problem of speculative metaphysics is only effectively defined, when the work of the descriptive metaphysician has been, to some extent at least, set in hand. In the first chapter of this book Aristotle and Kant were selected as 'foremost among the practitioners of descriptive metaphysics'; in later chapters we shall turn again in greater detail to the complexities of Kant's work, arguing that in him we have a remarkable example of a philosopher in whom both descriptive and speculative impulses are combined with a profound self-consciousness

[1] *Philosophical Review* ((Cornell), January 1965).

in respect of the assumptions and limits of both enterprises. For the present, however, I would invite the reader to attend to a very well-known passage from Plato's *Republic*, and to do so fully aware of the devastating criticism to which Aristotle submitted Plato's theory of forms in his *Metaphysics* (a criticism, indeed, anticipated by Plato himself in the *Parmenides*).

The passage is the very familiar one with which the two young men, Glaucon and Adeimantus, introduce the central ethical preoccupation of the whole dialogue. Here I quote from Cornford's translation.[2]

What people say is that to do wrong is, in itself, a desirable thing; on the other hand, it is not at all desirable to suffer wrong, and the harm to the sufferer outweighs the advantage to the doer. Consequently, when men have had a taste of both, those who have not the power to seize the advantage and escape the harm decide that they would be better off if they make a compact neither to do wrong nor to suffer it. Hence they began to make laws and covenants with one another; and whatever the law prescribed they called lawful and right. That is what right or justice is and how it came into existence; it stands half-way between the best thing of all – to do wrong with impunity – and the worst, which is to suffer wrong without the power to retaliate. So justice is accepted as a compromise, and valued, not as good in itself, but for lack of power to do wrong; no man worthy of the name, who had that power, would ever enter into such a compact with anyone; he would be mad if he did. That, Socrates, is the nature of justice according to this account, and such the circumstances in which it arose.

The next point is that men practise it against the grain, for lack of power to do wrong. How true that is, we shall best see if we imagine two men, one just, the other unjust, given full licence to do whatever they like, and then follow them to observe where each will be led by his desires. We shall catch the just man taking the same road as the unjust; he will be moved by self-interest, the end which it is natural to every creature to pursue as good, until forcibly turned aside by law and custom to respect the principle of equality.

Now, the easiest way to give them that complete liberty of action would be to imagine them possessed of the talisman

2 *Republic*. II. 358–61 (Cornford's translation, pp. 42–5).

found by Gyges, the ancestor of the famous Lydian. The story
tells how he was a shepherd in the King's service. One day
there was a great storm, and the ground where his flock was
feeding was rent by an earthquake. Astonished at the sight, he
went down into the chasm and saw, among other wonders of
which the story tells, a brazen horse, hollow, with windows in
its sides Peering in, he saw a dead body, which seemed to be
of more than human size. It was naked save for a gold ring,
which he took from the finger and made his way out. When the
shepherds met, as they did every month, to send an account to
the King of the state of his flocks, Gyges came wearing the ring.
As he was sitting with the others, he happened to turn the bezel
of the ring inside his hand. At once he became invisible, and his
companions, to his surprise, began to speak of him as if he had
left them. Then, as he was fingering the ring, he turned the
bezel outwards and became visible again. With that, he set
about testing the ring to see if it really had this power, and
always with the same result: according as he turned the bezel
inside or out he vanished and reappeared. After this discovery
he contrived to be one of the messengers sent to the court. There
he seduced the Queen, and with her help murdered the King and
seized the throne.

Now suppose there were two such magic rings, and one were
given to the just man, the other to the unjust. No one, it is
commonly believed, would have such iron strength of mind as
to stand fast in doing right or keep his hands off other men's
goods, when he could go to the market-place and fearlessly help
himself to anything he wanted, enter houses and sleep with any
woman he chose, set prisoners free and kill men at his pleasure,
and in a word go about among men with the powers of a god.
He would behave no better than the other; both would take the
same course. Surely this would be strong proof that men do right
only under compulsion; no individual thinks of it as good for
him personally, since he does wrong whenever he finds he has
the power. Every man believes that wrongdoing pays him personally much better, and, according to this theory, that is the
truth. Granted full licence to do as he liked, people would think
him a miserable fool if they found him refusing to wrong his
neighbours or to touch their belongings, though in public they
would keep up a pretence of praising his conduct, for fear of
being wronged themselves. So much for that.

Finally, if we are really to judge between the two lives, the only way is to contrast the extremes of justice and injustice. We can best do that by imagining our two men to be perfect types, and crediting both to the full with the qualities they need for their respective ways of life. To begin with the unjust man: he must be like any consummate master of a craft, a physician or a captain, who, knowing just what his art can do, never tries to do more, and can always retrieve a false step. The unjust man, if he is to reach perfection, must be equally discreet in his criminal attempts, and he must not be found out, or we shall think him a bungler; for the highest pitch of injustice is to seem just when you are not. So we must endow our man with the full complement of injustice; we must allow him to have secured a spotless reputation for virtue while committing the blackest crimes; he must be able to retrieve any mistake, to defend himself with convincing eloquence if his misdeeds are denounced, and, when force is required, to bear down all opposition by his courage and strength and by his command of friends and money.

Now set beside this paragon the just man in his simplicity and nobleness, one who, in Aeschylus' words, 'would be, not seem, the best'. There must, indeed, be no such seeming; for if his character were apparent, his reputation would bring him honours and rewards, and then we should not know whether it was for their sake that he was just, or for justice's sake alone. He must be stripped of everything but justice, and denied every advantage the other enjoyed. Doing no wrong, he must have the worse reputation for wrongdoing, to test whether his virtue is proof against all that comes of having a bad name; and under this life-long imputation of wickedness, let him hold on his course of justice unwavering to the point of death. And so, when the two men have carried their justice and injustice to the last extreme, we may judge which is the happier.

This passage introduces the famous comparison of the perfectly just with the perfectly unjust man, with which Plato crystallises the issue which he wishes to raise in the dialogue. The story of Gyges' ring is the story of what, it is alleged, every man in his heart would wish to be the case. We would all of us like to be able to ignore the laws of the society in which we live, including all moral laws and moral conventions, as well, of course, as the laws given positive effect by legislative and executive authority. We would all of us like to be able to go beyond the confines in which these traditions contain our desires and crib our secret aspirations. We do not attempt this because we know perfectly well that in the process we are liable to be hurt; we are dissuaded from the attempt by prudence. So we have to content ourselves with that *pis aller*, that second best, which an accepted system of morality sustains and promotes. In our fantasies, perhaps in our dreams, we think how wonderful it would be to find a ring which we could manipulate, and so, turning ourselves invisible at will, follow the promptings of our own desires. But we know that such rings are not likely to come our way; we are not the stuff of which demi-gods are made; we have to accept the contract of morality. But the dream – and I use the word advisedly – haunts us; and because we are haunted by it, we come to see the system of restraints under which we live as something that, even as we accept it, we regard as alienating or estranging ourselves from ourselves; under a system of conventional morality, we are no longer as we would be; we haven't the strength; the power to be so has not come our way; yet the recognition of our estrangement irritates and chafes us, and so we are at war with ourselves. To use again, in a quite different connection, the imagery invoked at the outset of this chapter: we thrust impotently against the barriers in which our common weakness contains us all, and crave for ourselves as individuals the strength which would permit a careful, all-conquering indulgence.

The insight of this passage is remarkable; but the lesson is more sharply pointed when Glaucon goes on to contrast two images of the good life; the first that of the perfectly unjust, the second that of the perfectly just man. Gyges is the example of the type of the perfectly unjust man, and as the argument proceeds we come to see that we make a great mistake if we suppose that the figure whom Glaucon has in mind is one who rides through power to a throne, an Attila, a 'scourge of God'. A man may do what Gyges did, and be judged by conventional standards very reprehensible; yet we have no reason to suppose that such a man, when once he had attained his throne, would do other than display himself the benefactor, even the servant, of those over whom he bears rule.

There is, of course, no doubt at all in this passage that Plato has in mind some of the darker sides of the Athenian achievement, the power-realities that made possible the glories of Athens in her supreme hour. If a man is to achieve power, he must use the resources put at his disposal quite ruthlessly; he must not be afraid to kill, even as Athens was not afraid under Pericles' leadership to convert the resources of the common treasury of the Delian Confederacy to her own advantage. And here, of course, advantage is not to be construed in any narrowly material sense; we are not to assume in understanding how the word is used, the acceptance of a Benthamite dogma of the homogeneity of satisfactions. Pericles knew very much more of the rich possibilities of human existence than his critics; yet he was realist enough to see that adequate human resources were the necessary conditions of their actualisation. What the Gyges's of this world have to their credit are, in fact, very often those positive achievements which make up what we normally regard as the more admirable parts of human history. Such men are not the 'scourges of God'; they are, for instance, the men whose courageous initiation of public works makes possible the full employment in essentially constructive activity of the man-power of their city; they also include (if I may translate into modern terms) the men whose generous endowment of temples and sacrifices receives high commendation for 'their service to the cause of Church extension'. They are the men of quick practical perception, sharp to notice moments of opportunity, and resolute in turning them to maximum advantage; so they 'gain the appearance of justice'. It is not, I believe, over-ingenious exegesis to recall, when we read this passage, the view of the status of 'appearance' we find in the later books of the *Republic*. 'Appearance' in those books is that which 'lies between being and not-being'; so the men of whom Glaucon is speaking are not to be written off as successful humbugs, who have effectively concealed the manner of their money-making operations, at least till long after their obituaries have been written. They are, in fact, very far from being the servants simply of their own will. In following their star they bring enormous benefit to others, and the high reputation that is theirs is not the reputation of the successful moral fraud; rather it is the reputation won in a hard school by a man of genuine and recognisable achievement, even if blessed by good fortune, which alone in the beginning and the end of the day, finally made the achievement possible.

Per contra, the image of the perfectly just man, the image with which Glaucon follows that of the perfectly unjust, is one of human failure. The perfectly just man is, of course, very much more than the man who fulfils completely the prescriptions of conventional morality, who 'has kept the commandments' from his youth up; rather he is the man who has interiorised the principles of such

22

morality, and is concerned before all else to purify his intentions and his motives. Such a man becomes perilously like the philosopher who, in the hour of Athens' mortal danger, seemed to counsel men to abstain from the moral risk of action, and so diminished, through the advice he gave, the collective will to resist; he sought personal purity of heart at the cost of the effect of his quest on the lives of his fellow citizens, and his quizzical scepticism concerning the validity of Athens' cause wore away resolution, and undermined commitment. Just as the Gyges's of this world are the men who contribute most to human welfare, so the perfectly just men are very often those who, by their scrupulosity, by their subtle agnosticism, by their concern with the ideal, imperil and help to destroy the excellent, even the humanly decent, in the name of the supposedly perfect. Of course, it is very hard to avoid here the sense of the contrast between Pericles and Socrates, as Plato saw them. It is, indeed, the presence of this contrast in the author's mind which makes it so important for the right understanding of the passage that we do not consider the perfectly unjust man as a successful humbug. The portrayal of Gyges in the myth enables us both to perceive more clearly the depth of the opposition between perfectly unjust and perfectly just, and prepares our minds for what Plato would have us take seriously – the case for the perfectly unjust man.

It may seem that I have spent a very long time on a passage very familiar to any student of philosophy, and that I have had very little, if anything, new to say about it. Yet I have done this quite deliberately. In this early part of the *Republic* the dialogue-form is still something very much alive. It is not yet stylised. As we read the words of the two young men, we seem to be overhearing a real conversation. So Adeimantus adds his lengthy footnote to Glaucon's presentation of his viewpoint, complementing his brother's argument with a vivid evocation of his education (in the sense of *paideia* or *Bildung*). He shows himself aware how all that he has overheard in the environment of his youth has conditioned him to take seriously the claim of the perfectly unjust man to represent the true norm of human life. In the end, he says that he has heard success praised more than integrity, effectiveness on the plane of power extolled above purity of heart, etc. Success brings reputation for virtue in its train. Men are indeed encouraged to practise virtue; but this only because that way lies the only road to success open to most of us. A man may need to practise honesty to secure his own advancement; but it is the latter which exercises unconditional authority; and whatever men may say from platforms, or from pulpits, in the secret places of their hearts, and indeed on the occasions when they feel free uninhibitedly to express and reveal their inmost hopes, it is by success (a state we all of us can recognise), and not by scrupulosity, by effectiveness and not by inward integrity, that we measure and judge a man's achievement.

At this stage, I repeat, in the *Republic* we are invited to listen to actual conversation. Later the exposition becomes much more formal, and the importance of the use of the dialogue-form is minimal; but at this stage, every sentence counts. It is relevant comment here to quote the remark of the French Catholic philosopher, Maurice Blondel – 'Human life is metaphysics in action.' Indeed I want to suggest that this whole passage, on part of which I have now commented in some detail, is an example of the kind of metaphysics that we often see realised when men half-committed or more than half-committed to particular policies or directions of human life, become articulate and questioning concerning their validity. At first sight, to speak of the young men's request as itself a piece of metaphysics may seem paradoxical in view of the fact that the transcendent ontology in the central books of the *Republic* is offered as part of an answer to the request which these young men put forward. To characterise the request itself as a piece of metaphysics may seem to make the extraordinary mistake of identifying the request with the answer that is later given to it. To this charge I plead not guilty, only suggesting that if we are to understand aright the transcendent ontology of Books V to VII we must at all times bear in mind the nature of the deep scepticism it is concerned to lay to rest. To this matter I shall return later; for the time being I should like briefly to fasten on the passage in Book VI in which, shortly before the exposition of the doctrine of the idea of the Good, by way of the analogy of the sun, Socrates characterises that Good as that which every man pursues and makes the end of all his actions, having a presentiment, indeed, that there is such an end, yet enjoying concerning it no confident opinion, only sure that here is a matter of such importance that nothing but an absolute certainty should content him. In the conversation which I have been discussing, we should surely see *just that pursuit in action*. It is a phase of the restless quest that we are invited to enter into, a phase with which the climactic intellectual experience of the secondary education is continuous.

Glaucon and Adeimantus are presented as men who have 'seen through' traditional morality. The cake of custom has been broken for them; they are sophisticated enough to appreciate the need of finding the sanctions of that morality in the sort of life it promotes. Their evaluation of that authority is utilitarian; but it is an evaluation in pessimistic utilitarian terms, the terms of Thomas Hobbes rather than those of Jeremy Bentham or James Mill. For whereas an optimistic utilitarian will say that the restraints and directives of traditional morality, in so far as they are valid, help to promote human happiness, and to throw wide the doors to a richer life for all, the pessimistic utilitarian will only urge that these restraints and directives at least keep and deter men from the courses of action likely to issue only in mutual destruction. The mood of the two young men, particularly Glaucon, is pessimistic. For them traditional morality is a *pis aller*, yet there is a sense in which their scepticism is more directed towards the attitudes that have replaced the traditional estimation of traditional morality, than to that traditional estimate itself. In the opposition of perfectly just and perfectly unjust men, their uncertainty achieves a radical expression. At the level of that opposition we have moved beyond the question of the status of traditional morality; we ask which of two ways of life, realised concretely in different individuals, has the root of the human matter in it. Glaucon is not absolutely sure that Pericles in the end has the edge on Socrates. Only someone who has moved beyond the mere issue of the vindication of traditional morality could articulate the sort of metaphysical perplexities which are raised by the opposition of the two patterns of human life. And it is highly significant that these patterns are not presented schematically, but with a wealth of detail sufficient to show the extent to which it is in the concrete of actual moral and political choice that the metaphysical problem is raised: and this because human life, especially when informed by a certain degree of self-conscious awareness, if not 'metaphysics in action' (unless the term metaphysics is used as a synonym for *Weltanschauung*) is at least a place where the problem of metaphysics is set, and the question of its possibility most sharply raised.

So the young men show themselves already metaphysically minded when they set over against each other the perfectly unjust and the perfectly just man. Further, in the form in which we find this in Plato, we are already made aware of the extent to which the metaphysically-minded 'thrust at the limits of language'. One may find the transcendent ontology of the central section of the *Republic* either unintelligible, or incredible, or both; or one may try to salvage from it certain logical insights which, in the form in which they are

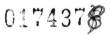

presented, are overlaid by the author's ethical and speculative fantasies. Of this I have already said something, and shall have more to add later. But what I want to emphasise now is the significance of the kind of groping which is articulated in this stretch of dialogue.

Dialogue is not, of course, directly descriptive. Yet if one asks whether this piece of dialogue is true or false, (and although one seems here to be asking a question which is badly framed, involving a breach of 'category-fittingness' in the way in which it is propounded, one also seems to be asking a genuine question), one must be able significantly to ask whether a dialogue represents what is the case, whether a dialogue, or a conversation for that matter, enables one to draw nearer to what is the case. One can go further and ask whether something which is the case may not be something which can find its proper 'system of projection' in this way, and in no other way. In the memoir of Wittgenstein by Professor Norman Malcolm and Professor G. H. von Wright, it is suggested that Wittgenstein broke with the picture theory of the proposition, developed in the *Tractatus*, when his friend, the economic historian, Dr Piero Sraffa, carried out, in his presence, a traditional Neapolitan gesture of contempt, and asked him whether it was in any sense a picture of reality. Now I would wish to claim that there is a sense, or even that there are senses, in which one could claim that this conversation, this dialogue, *was itself a proposition*, though hardly in any ordinary sense a picture of reality.[3] Indeed, one has to say just that, if one wishes to thrust on one's attention, and keep before one's attention, what is absolutely central in the problem of metaphysics, namely the question of the truth or falsity of a piece of metaphysics. Of course, one may judge the conversation worth listening to; of course, it is an impressive piece of Greek prose, making articulate the perplexities of these two young men, expressing their aspirations, revealing the restlessness of their hearts till they find rest in the Good. (But restlessness of heart is not by itself evidence that there is the Good in which the restless heart may find rest; a very different sort of therapy may be required.) One can say all this without raising the absolutely crucial question whether or not in this sort of discourse we draw nearer to what is the case, whether or not something is being represented in this sort of discourse that is there to be represented.

It is not uncommon today for those concerned to establish the possibility of metaphysical discourse to avail themselves of a principle of tolerance formulated in the language of Professor John Wisdom –

[3] See chapter 6, pp. 73ff.

'Every sort of statement has its own sort of logic.' No doubt it has; but it remains true that it only has its sort of logic if it is indeed a statement. The conversation or dialogue to which this chapter is devoted only has its own sort of logic if, indeed, it is properly designated a proposition or statement, if it intends reference to what is the case. Now Plato beyond question thought that such reference was intended, and much of the *Republic* is devoted to a programmatic account of the way in which men may perfect their intellectual grasp of that towards which these young men are depicted as groping their way. Professor Antony Andrewes, in his study of *The Greek Tyrants*[4] notes that the earliest surviving use of the word *turannos* in Greek literature is in a fragment of Archilochus referring to Gyges, and he suggests that this may be absolutely the earliest use of the word. Readers of the *Republic* are well aware that when, in Book IX, we reach the image of the tyrannical man, we are, in fact, being given the picture of Gyges as he is seen by men who, through philosophical education, are enabled to see him as he is. Much of the *Republic* is concerned with the kind of training that men must undergo if they are to correct the educational perversion suspected by Adeimantus, and if they are to validate by working out to the full the suspicions to which Glaucon and he give expression. We may find the positive metaphysical doctrine of the *Republic* totally unacceptable; yet if we see it as an attempt to fulfil the demands of this introductory conversation, and seek to assess it as such, we may be moved to attempt a more profound judgement on the whole enterprise of which it is part. We are today, however, very much more immediately at home with the kind of discourse in which the young men set out their discontent, than with the exposition offered in Plato's consistent attempt to allay that discontent. Indeed, if we make anything at all of the latter, we do so only in relation to the former, taking it even as a kind of continuation of the *malaise* which Plato hopes it will dissipate. The problem that faces us is that of assessing the kind of validity which we may give to such crystallisation of discontent, of understanding how such discourse relates to other forms of discourse, above all how such discourse can fulfil the condition of being in a measure descriptive and referential.

In later chapters reference will be made to the fundamental opposition in the theory of knowledge, between what I there call 'realism', and what I there call 'constructivism' (the latter term is borrowed from the philosophy of mathematics). Let us now apply

[4] *Hutchinson Universal Library* (1956).

these terms to the passage which has provided the theme of the present chapter. If we are thorough-going constructivists, I suppose we could say that the man's groping was an end in itself. If we say this we say something important, in as much as this stretch of dialogue is the concretion of a metaphysical experience. If in any sense we understand it, we understand the young men's situation. Certainly, if we are concerned to explore the problem of metaphysics, we must not turn aside from the hermeneutics of metaphysical experience, and it is as the fragment of such experience that we have been concerned with the conversation of Glaucon and Adeimantus. We must not allow our attention to be deflected from the ways in which such experience is articulated, from the use of the dialogue-form, from the invocation of examples, from the intrusion of the concrete, etc. For in metaphysical experience we have to do with an aspect of the human situation, an aspect of men's coming to terms with their environment, in this case with their moral environment. But that there is such experience *de facto* does not, of course, in any sense establish that it is valid *de jure*. We may say that the world would be a poorer place without these discontents; we may even, as utilitarians, find a role for them in the promotion of the betterment of human kind. So Mill himself, in his *Essay on Liberty*, pleaded eloquently that we should not suppress the eccentric, the asker of awkward questions, lest by so doing we might diminish the range of opportunity which his interrogation might open to us. Thus one might offer a *quasi-utilitarian* justification of metaphysical discontent as something which can be positive in its fruits, as something which, if properly assimilated, can be delivered from the sterility which threatens it. To do this is only to engage tangentially with the question of truth and falsity; it is not to ask the question how far this kind of discourse is in any sense representative of what is the case.

We cannot therefore go the whole way with the constructivists. Although they tempt us by the suggestion that metaphysical insight is something which men may significantly create or bring into being for themselves, yet if there is anything worthy to be called metaphysical insight, then whatever the form in which it is expressed, it is a finding of what is the case; it is discovery, rather than creation. (I am deliberately using here highly general terms, with whose elucidation subsequent chapters will be concerned.) To emphasise the element of discovery in this way is not to diminish the importance of attending in detail to the forms that metaphysical experience may assume, and to other forms at once akin to it, and yet significantly different from it. We have to understand the metaphysician if we would understand what metaphysics is; but to understand the metaphysician is not by itself to validate the metaphysical enterprise. For that enterprise, whether speculative or descriptive, is concerned in the end with what is the case. It would have been no consolation to Glaucon and Adeimantus simply to have been praised – they would have rightly suspected the irony of such commendation – for their devotion to ideals, or for their obstinate adherence to their aspirations. What they were concerned with was an issue which can only be expressed in terms of the correspondence conception of truth. When we grope, when we articulate our gropings, bending concepts to novel service in their articulation, do the propositions which we frame and entertain agree in any sense with what is the case? And if so, what is it with which they agree or disagree? Whatever else we may say on the subject of Plato's own metaphysic, as developed in the *Republic*, we have to allow that he did take seriously the question of truth and falsity; he did not suppose that spiritual experience (including under that rubric the kind of quizzical self-interrogation exemplified in the conversation of Glaucon and Adeimantus) was an end in itself; it was authentic only so far as in it men were seeking what was the case.

The significance of the contribution made by the *Republic* to ethics is in danger of being overlooked because of the many faults of Plato's political theory.[5] It is, after all, not uncommon for a man who is most successful as a moral philosopher to come badly to grief in exploring the principles of politics. Plato is here a classically awful example; but this does not by itself diminish his achievement as a moralist. Part of that achievement lay in the boldness with which, in the comparison of lives in the *Republic*, he defended the thesis that one form of life was highest, because it most corresponded with what was the case, because it most captured the likeness of the actual. He'd compared lives on a scale by reference to their departure from that greatest approximation, that most nearly complete embodiment of the real. It may seem strange to speak in this way of correspondence, where forms of life are concerned. If Plato does so, (and I think he does), in doing so he gives free rein to the depth of his realism, to his conviction that if the metaphysically-minded attitude was to be justified, it could only be because in the articulation of that attitude

---

[5] The passage we have been concerned with is indeed relevant to Plato's political theory; but he could have drawn consequences from it for that theory incompatible with not a little of its substance!

we were groping towards what is the case. The exposition of what it is to be metaphysically minded is intermittent. On occasion, as in the passage with which this chapter has been mainly concerned, he is extraordinarily pregnant and illuminating; for here he offers a kind of exemplary exposé of the approach to metaphysics by way of ethics, seeing and capturing the kind of ethical reflection that is all the time inchoately metaphysical. In this passage it is not accidental that he is extraordinarily vivid on the plane of concrete example. If we go beyond him, it must be by the use of further examples concerned to bring out other ways in which this same, and other similar moods, express themselves. Yet, like Plato, we shall be well advised to realise that such moods are only significant if their expression forces on us the question of the truth or falsity of what is thus expressed. These moods are in themselves first and foremost moods and their expression is not self-authenticating. This last we must emphasise though we may have to see that *without just such expression* discoveries we hope to make would go unachieved.

3

Metaphysics and fact

The first section of this chapter will be devoted to the notion of fact. Freud, says Professor Eysenck, in characteristic mood, 'never had any notion of what is meant by fact in scientific discussion'. This remark will do as well as any other as a starting-point. Certainly the notion of fact has been extensively discussed in recent philosophy. I should like to distinguish two phases in that discussion, and to comment briefly upon them; the reader who is well-informed about the subsequent development of the argument will notice where I stop; but he will perhaps draw his own conclusions from my breaking off where I do.

1. In the early years of this century there was a revival of interest in the notion of fact, which followed the development in the closely related logical and epistemological work of G. E. Moore and Bertrand Russell, of a sustained criticism of the idealist identification of truth with an all-embracing, internally consistent unitary system of judgements, and the consequent identification of error as the investing with the character of unconditional validity, of individual affirmations, which could at best claim only a partial truth. In criticism of this doctrine there was an effective revival and restatement of the classical correspondence conception of truth, according to which a true proposition was one which corresponded with a fact. But this revival did not content itself simply with the reaffirmation of a view which holds irresistible attraction for common sense (in spite of the great difficulties involved in working it out in detail); it extended into an interest in the so-called 'structure of facts', in the manner of their complex, relational unity, whereby the fact, for instance, that *Cassius hated Caesar* was differentiated from the fact *Caesar hated Cassius*.[1] These investigations belonged very intimately to the sort of philosophising which is commonly referred to by the title 'logical atomism' and although its underlying impulse included in part a

---

[1] The 'direction' of the hatred is different in the two facts mentioned.

rejection of the spiritualistic monism characteristic of the British idealists, a microscopic investigation of the structure and constitution of
the facts the world contained (and which, according to some philosophers, made up its fundamental stuff) involved technical discussions
which went far beyond the rehabilitation of the commonsensical.

2. Here, however, it should be noticed that philosophers who were
by no means committed to the rigours of a thorough-going logical
atomist programme, were to this extent in sympathy with that programme; – that in so far as they professed any sort of metaphysic
that metaphysic could best be characterised as a thorough-going
pluralistic realism. In this connection we may refer to the late
Professor G. H. Hardy's Rouse-Ball lecture on *Mathematical Proof*.[2]
Professor Hardy is an outstanding example of a pure mathematician,
who regarded the work of the pure mathematician as a form of discovery, and not of invention. (Here I refer to the distinction between
invention and discovery, with which I shall be often concerned in
later chapters of this work.) Thus (if I understand Hardy's argument
correctly), if there were a rigorous proof of the theorem that any
even number is the sum of two primes, by that proof something
would have been discovered necessarily to be the case, that is
eternally so, even if the whole history of the world were totally
different. Indeed, Hardy was ready to use the image of the discovery
of the details of a continent by an explorer, which has previously only
been roughly mapped out, to convey the character of the mathematician's experience. As in the case of the continent, whose detail
remains relatively unknown until it is actually crossed by the
explorer, so the sector of mathematical reality with which the mathematician is concerned, remains unknown in the detail of its structural
order, until his proof is complete. Of course there are certainly enormous differences between the procedures followed, and the experiences enjoyed by pure mathematicians, on the one hand, and
explorers on the other. Indeed, if I understand Hardy aright, for him
the main purpose of the analogy is to insist against the constructivist,
on the view that the mathematician does not *create* his own world.

Again we are certainly justified in using the term 'external relation' to indicate the way in which Hardy and others see the
relation between what is proved when such a theorem is proved,
and what is the case when I say, for instance, that it rained in Portree
on 6 August 1966. Thus, if it is true that any even number is the
sum of two primes (and if this is true it is, of course, necessarily

[2] *Mind* (1929).

true), this remains the case, even if the weather in Portree on the day in question had been totally different. One could go further and remark that the entire history of Western Europe, from Charlemagne to the present, might have been totally different, and yet the state of affairs in mathematics remain necessarily as it is. Something of this kind was undoubtedly suggested by Plato; but when the view was reactivated by philosophers at the turn of the century (some of whom, especially Russell, were intensely concerned with questions relating to the status of mathematics), they were presented as part of a general ultimate pluralism; that is a doctrine content to affirm in the world the reality of a number of mutually irreducible, ultimately different sorts of fact, enjoying indeed, in respect of their nature, such independence, one of another, that one could conceive a world containing some of them, but in which others would be altogether lacking.

3. Further, in this connection mention should be made of a very important type of philosophical argument, used to great effect by Professor G. E. Moore. This argument takes the shape of challenging the student to ask himself whether, in fact, he is not more sure that some common-sensical proposition is true (e.g. some proposition relating to the behaviour of unobserved, and indeed hardly observable, physical objects), than that some general philosophical theory, (e.g. the inevitably paradoxical phenomenalistic reconstruction of the constituents of the physical world) should be adopted as a final and comprehensive account of reality. This sort of argument, used on occasion by Moore with devastating effect, clearly takes for granted that we do know, beyond shadow of question, certain states of affairs to be the case, and that we do know certain isolated facts. It is most important to recognise that we are not here concerned with any kind of 'hard data' (usually illustrated by the supposed immediate deliverances of sense-awareness, emphasised by classic empiricist philosophers), but with such states of affairs as *the world has existed for a great many years before I was born*, which would not for one moment be questioned by ordinary people. If the selection of candidates for inclusion in this list of alleged certainties seems sometimes random, and sometimes expressive of a lack of historical imagination (a criticism sharply made by the late Professor R. G. Collingwood), the cutting effectiveness of the citation of such examples in criticism of pretentious metaphysical speculation remains.

4. In the 1930s, the term *fact* became, in philosophical discussion, a synonym for that which verifies, confirms, or falsifies a hypothesis;

the word, indeed, became a label for the deliverance of observation in so far as such deliverance established or invalidated claims concerning what was the case. If, in the previous phases of this discussion, the term had had primarily ontological import, in this second phase the emphasis was epistemological.

It is not my purpose here or elsewhere to attempt to summarise the long discussions concerning the 'verification principle'; and the gradual modifications that principle underwent from the moment of its first bold formulation as *the meaning of a proposition is the method of its verification*, to the later efforts to establish the claims of some so-called 'weak verification' principle. What I wish, however, to suggest is that those empiricists who made effective use of this maxim in the first instance, to eliminate from scientific theory reference to that which was recognised as unobservable in principle, whose role could therefore be shown to be purely otiose, and then to extend to the whole body of human knowledge a corresponding economy and discipline in respect of the dispensable and supposititious, were operating with a concept of fact which identified the factual with the observable. A fact was that which was observably the case; the category of fact was, indeed, an epistemological, as distinct from an ontological, category. Those readers who are familiar with the sort of philosophical discussion carried on in *Mind*, and in the *Proceedings of the Aristotelian Society* during the 1930s will know how many of them were concerned with the viability of a phenomenalist programme in respect of our knowledge of the external world, the viability that is of a programme which sought to reduce all that we said or claimed to be able to say about the world around us, whether at the level of everyday life, or of scientific description and theory, to statements concerning actual and possible observations. One of the sources of the programme's inspiration was undoubtedly the conviction that when one was dealing with what one saw, heard, smelt, tasted, touched, then one's feet were secure on the ground, and the impulse to speculate, to weave patterns of theoretical construction which commended themselves on grounds of their alleged self-evidence, or on the authority of their quasi-aesthetic appeal, received effective discipline. In respect of the first use of the concept of fact mentioned above, it was made clear that however seriously logical pluralists might discuss aspects of this programme, (and it is well known how much time Professor Moore gave to examination of the phenomenalist theory of our knowledge of the external world), they did not identify the factual with the observable.

34

For instance, they were prepared to allow as a view meriting most serious discussion, the doctrine that mathematical equations were facts, (the view which Hardy held), even if they were completely agnostic concerning the possibility of saying more concerning the relation of these facts to the facts of the history of the natural world, than that a complete account of the sorts of fact there are in the universe must make mention of both of them. This kind of onto-logical tolerance was alien to the champions of the verification principle, who sought rather to include in a general treatment of necessary truth as 'true by convention', the whole field with which the pure mathematician was concerned.

What I would emphasise here is that with the discussion of the verification principle, the nuance of the notion of fact changed significantly; yet I would argue that both the use of the notion by the logical pluralists, and its later use by the verificationists, reflected something highly significant in the varied use of the term. Where we claim to be dealing with facts, we have our feet firmly on the ground. To the pluralists the fundamental error of the idealists was that of neglecting the obvious and certain in the interests of the precariously woven and hardly attainable; and clearly allied to this mistake was the associated refusal to allow that the world included a large num-ber of ontologically distinguishable sorts of categories of existents, and to accept that we did most certainly enjoy, where some of them were concerned, clear knowledge about them, which was not in-validated by its inevitable incompleteness, or by the fact that we had to acknowledge ourselves still in the dark where an enormous number of other things were concerned. Similarly, the radical empiri-cist was always quick to insist that observation could definitely teach us concerning what is the case, and that we have resources at our disposal for answering questions concerning the way the world is, and indeed concerning the most fundamental laws that govern the behaviour of its constituents. For the verificationist, the category of fact is fundamentally epistemological; indeed for him the theory of knowledge is the most fundamental part of philosophy. The task of that theory is indeed to extend over the whole corpus of human know-ledge concerning what is the case, the sovereignty of the appeal to observation.

Now in the history of the 'verification principle', the publication in 1934 of the first edition of Professor Sir Karl Popper's *Logik der Forschung*, marked a very important moment. It is clearly recognised today that this work, with its implied criticism of much of the programme of traditional inductive logic, is very much more than a contribution to the controversies about the 'verification principle'. It represented a most serious attempt to emancipate empiricist theory of knowledge from its bondage to the dogma that the complex must always be capable of exhibition as a function of the simple, and that human knowledge must be shown to advance through generalisation from the colligation of a multitude of particular instances, etc. It sought to find room for creativity, for speculation, for the work of constructive imagination, even insisting that their role was sheerly indispensable in extension of our knowledge of the world. But it also insisted on the crucial distinction between a speculation that was a law unto itself, and which claimed an inalienable sovereignty in the following of its own prompting, and one that insisted that its most attractive suggestions should be vulnerable to refutation or falsification at the bar of observation. What Popper, in fact, seeks to establish is the differentia between the kind of speculation that is vital to theory-building, and the kind of speculation that by its deliberate self-emancipation from any sort of control by sense observation, forfeits the claim to be regarded as a serious essay in human discovery. If the phenomenalist seeks to extend throughout the whole corpus of human knowledge the sovereignty of the appeal to observation, those who follow Popper's path may be regarded as assigning to observation a role akin to that exercised by the American Supreme Court in disallowing legislation as unconstitutional. Here again the nuance of the notion of fact is epistemological; the force of the expression is conveyed when we speak of 'rubbing our noses in the facts'; of submitting the fruits of our theoretical construction to the test of observed fact, etc. We may, indeed, here think ourselves to be much nearer in temper to aspects of Kant's theory of knowledge, with its emphasis on putting nature to the question, rather than to the realism that sometimes in a very naive form was professed by the pluralists, or indeed to the besetting desire to exhibit the complex as a function of the epistemologically simple, that we find among empiricists.

Yet I would suggest that in the movement of epistemological thought which I have sketched, for all its most significant differences from the ontological discussions with which I was earlier concerned, there is discernible an analogous insistence on the underlying emphasis of the correspondence theory of truth, namely that when a proposition concerning the world is true, its truth is constituted by its correspondence with an external state of affairs. (It will be clear from other parts of this book that I recognise it as in a measure para-doxical to speak of a 'correspondence theory of truth' in connection with Kant! Yet it is possibly an enlightening paradox.) Our beliefs may sometimes be self-authenticated; that is, they may find con-firmation only through our taking the risk of embracing them; for instance, a man may only be able to confirm his belief that he will recover from an illness by believing that he will, and thereby establishing a necessary, if not a sufficient, condition for his recovery. But what authenticates such a belief, and indeed all beliefs, that we may hold concerning the world around us, are states of affairs exter-nal to those beliefs, on which, whether directly or indirectly, we seek by thinking to gain some sort of purchase-hold.

At first sight it may seem strange to preface an enquiry touching on the relation of ethics and metaphysics by this epistemological sketch. Yet we do well at the outset of such a discussion to remind ourselves of the notion of fact. It is especially relevant to the topic of ethical naturalism with which I am here particularly concerned. The distinguished French Platonic scholar, the late M. Léon Robin, in his book, *La Morale Antique*, wrote of Plato's ethics as 'un naturisme d'un type peu connu'. Now Robin is surely entirely justi-fied in speaking of the ethics of the *Republic* (with an aspect of which we were concerned in the last chapter) as 'naturalistic'; it is, indeed, fundamental to Plato's argument that the secrets of the world are in the last resort only revealed to the saint, and that moral perfection itself is secured by the intellectual penetration it alone makes possible.

For Plato, as much as for Bentham, what men ought to do, the way in which they ought to live their lives, sprang out of the way in which things are; in some sense (as we saw in the last chapter) their lives *correspond* with the order of being and becoming.

It is fascinating indeed to compare Plato's procedure with that followed by the most rigorous servant of a thorough-going natur-alistic 'programme in ethics', Jeremy Bentham. The latter sought, as far as possible, to eliminate the notion of 'ought' from the language: to extend the sovereignty of the actual over the ideal, to the point of submerging the latter altogether under the former. 'Poetry is mis-representation.' In this formula there is summarised the very heart of the Benthamite *credo* with its unflinching resolution to have done with all that might deflect human beings from adopting any other norms of behaviour than those demonstrably effective in advancing the maximum possible satisfaction. In such a view there was as little place for any attempt to establish criteria of satisfaction as there was for the suggestion that the scrupulosity of the morally sensitive, especially if it interrupted the smooth progress of the cause of human welfare, or disturbed the accepted canons of the permissible, could be regarded as somehow self-authenticating. When Bentham notoriously insisted that 'all desire is for pleasure', he was less proposing as foundation of his ethical system an obviously false empirical generalisation than expressing in a misleading way his repudiation of the search for a criterion of satisfactions as a completely vacuous pursuit.

For Plato, on the other hand, this search belonged to the very heart of the moral philosopher's task; it was indeed identified by him with the metaphysical pilgrimage whose route he sought to trace in the account given in the *Republic* of the 'secondary education'. The form he gives to this intellectual journey is, however, unmistakable evidence of his underlying sympathy with the radical empiricists' insistence that there shall be no disregarding of the sovereignty of concern with what is the case, and no indulgence of romantic fancy as if, by itself, such an aspiration could deliver men from the need of an ultimate seriousness concerning what is and what is not the case.

Where Plato and the Benthamites agree is in their insistence that at the *ultimate* level the moral philosopher is concerned with what is the case: that the way in which we live our lives, even the sharpness with which the question how we should do so presses on us, imposes a veto on any sort of light-hearted disregard of questions concerning the ways in which things are. Morality is not a matter of arbitrary choice; it is in some sense expressive, at the level of human action, of the order of the world.

I began this chapter with a characteristic quotation from Professor Eysenck on the subject of Freud. No one who in this controversy is convinced that Freud is right will dispute that what Eysenck is saying amounts in the end to no more than a disguised rebuke that the founder of psychoanalysis was not a behaviourist. No doubt it is true that for Eysenck the behaviourists alone among psychologists have a proper understanding of what is meant by fact in scientific discussion. But the temper expressed in his rebuke must be reckoned with by anyone concerned with interpretation in depth of the travail of the human spirit, for instance of human obstinacy in affirmation of the often-conflicting principles of justice and compassion, of integrity and pity. What seems so inescapably clear to an allegedly unchallengeable introspection may also very quickly assume the character of a mere casual byplay on the surface of existence. The most intimate self-interrogation, the most emotionally and imaginatively costly self-scrutiny, the precarious achievement of a hauntingly genuine humility that is not the mere substitution of a catastrophic self-laceration for a punctured pride – all these experiences assume quickly the highly questionable status of the subjective and capricious. If we are honest we must acknowledge the possibility that such experience is mere empty expense of time and energy that are better directed to a more disciplined, less spiritually pretentious promotion of validly ascertainable, obviously recognisable human welfare. A question is set against the factual import of metaphysical perplexity, in particular against that sort of metaphysical perplexity which gives shape to the kind of self-scrutiny to which I have referred, to that time-consuming, besetting concern with an ultimate integrity which involves at once a victory over insinuating self-regard, and over that false scrupulosity which abstains from the risk of action, in the name of purity of motive.

In the last chapter I spoke of the 'thrust against the limits of language'. We are now engaged with the extension of the concept of fact, where fact is understood as that which confirms or falsifies, and as that which establishes itself as part of the furniture of the world. There would be no problem of metaphysics if the anti-metaphysical case were one which could be disposed of by a dexterous dismissal of the need to concern oneself with what is, or is not the case, where the foundation assumptions of human existence are at issue. We shall see later the extent to which radical empiricism mediates a kind of ethical liberation, a liberation, admittedly, which issues itself in its own peculiar sort of bondage, but a liberation in as much as it sets the imagination free from seemingly sterile fantasy, and directs it towards the conception of viable policies of human betterment. But at present it is less with the ethical claim of the empiricist outlook that we are concerned, than with the urgency with which the empiricist emphasises the authority of fact. We must establish some kind of analogy between our commerce with the transcendent, and our commerce with the world about us. The proper characterisation of this analogy is the very heart of the problem of metaphysics, and we shall find that in the attempt to delineate it there is no substitute for hard work, perhaps no finality of assured attainment. But if we begin by asking whether the notion of observed fact is as simple as the logical empiricists, drawing perhaps more than they allow from the work of the logical atomists, suggest to us, we do so because the notion of fact is one of inescapable significance, and because it is only if we establish statements concerning the transcendent, as possessing some sort of intelligible factual import, that we need to bother ourselves with them at all.

To continue: we are speaking of learning facts. A man may say that he learns more about lust from Shakespeare's *Sonnets* than from essays on sexual morality, whether written from the humanist or the religious standpoint. We say, in this case, that he learns facts, and he comes perhaps to reject his previous policies and attitudes. Again, take quite a different example. At Bishopthorpe, it is possible to see the late Sir William Orpen's portrait of the late Cosmo Gordon Lang, as Archbishop of York. It was of that portrait that Archbishop Söderblöm of Sweden remarked that 'the artist has painted him as the devil intended him to be: but by the grace of God he is not like that'. No one who has seen that portrait at Bishopthorpe, or even the photogravure reproduction which forms the frontispiece of the late Mr J. G. Lockhart's life of *Cosmo Gordon Lang*[3] would deny that if this portrait is not a radical falsification of its subject, the viewer learns from it about the Archbishop that which it is not possible to learn from a multitude of photographs, however accurate they may be. It is logically possible that the portrait is a radical falsification of its subject; if we are to allow that it may teach us concerning its subject, we must allow that we may be misled. There is no infallible guarantee that delivers us from the task of confirming the lessons we have learnt; in this case confirming them by documentary evidence. Yet, as in the case of the *Sonnets*, so in that of the portrait, our perceptions are taken further; new tests are set them that otherwise they might well have avoided. There is the possibility of loss; yet also of very great gain.

Again take a more complex example, namely Shakespeare's tragedy of *Julius Caesar*. The play, of course, draws largely on Plutarch's lives of Caesar and of Brutus, lives whose historical value, and the historical value of whose sources, are matters for professional Roman historians; (although it is not unknown for writers on Roman history, discussing Caesar's position in the crucial months before his murder, and his intentions after his return from his projected Parthian campaign, to pay some attention to what Shakespeare says, and this because, although Shakespeare was not an historian, either in the sense of the modern Roman historian or in that of Plutarch,

[3] (Hodder and Stoughton, 1949.)

he was a man of tremendous insight). When Mr R. H. S. Crossman reviewed in the *Observer* the fascinating study by Mr Roger Manvell and Mr Heinrich Fraenkel of the plot against Hitler on 20 July 1944, he said there was one work, and one only known to him in the literature of British political thought, which really bore on the predicament of the brave men who sought to rid Germany of the monster, Adolf Hitler, and that work was Shakespeare's *Julius Caesar*. If one rereads the tragedy as a commentary on Manvell's study and other studies and records of the anti-Nazi conspiracy, one sees, or thinks one sees, many things which one had not noticed before. Again, the lessons one learnt, or believes one has learnt, are not simply restricted to that particular episode; they press down on the stuff of human life itself. There is the episode of the conspiracy, there is the interpretative commentary provided by a play that is itself an interpretation of a great historical episode, and there are the lessons learnt. One faces the problem of metaphysics when one asks concerning the lessons learnt, and the means whereby they are taught, the following questions. What sorts of lessons are these? How are they taught? How are they to be evaluated? There is, for the philosopher, the *de facto* reality of the exploration of human life, which is provided through the application of Shakespeare's tragedy to the illumination of a recent historical episode. There is also the question *Quid juris?*, the question of the justification of this exploration, of this claim to learn, and to have learnt. This is the problem to which I have referred continually in this chapter, and in the preceding, in speaking of the factual import of attempted exploration of the ultimate; and it is to this question that I shall return in the fifth chapter, when I ask the reader to direct his attention again to aspects of Kant's work.[4]

To develop the example more closely, we might contrast Brutus' hesitation, his uncertainty manifested in his conversations with Cassius and with Portia before lending his support to the plot being hatched against the life of one man, with the quick, resolute, almost detached and quizzical enterprise of the triumvirs. The latter figure in a very short scene, and while in the presentation of Brutus we are admitted to the deep bewilderment of a man pushed to and fro by conflicting impulses, in the presentation of the triumvirs we confront men who know exactly what they are about. Yet Brutus' scrupulosity marks a dishonesty of which we cannot, for instance,

[4] I refer to Kant's doctrine of the primacy of the practical reason to which I shall turn in chapter 5.

accuse Antonius in his determination to include Cicero in the list of those proscribed, or indeed in all the determined executants of effective vengeance in that merciless scene. They know what they are about; even the young Octavius is able to call a spade a spade. But Brutus' integrity and gentleness, and indeed his love for Caesar, drive him to a position in which he must seek to disguise from himself the real nature of what he is about; so he will characterise the murderous act as the ritual purification of the city, hiding from himself what it is to shed a man's life-blood in an act of assassination, by suggesting that it is the blood of a sacrifice which pours from Caesar's wounds. Here is deep tragedy, the tragedy of a man betrayed into self-deception, as well as into the ineffectiveness with which Cassius charges him by the very nobility of spirit which sets him apart from the triumvirs. But it is they, in their quick, philistine, yet skilful brutality, who are his superiors on the plane of action; because the mould in which they are cast is of more common clay, they are less vulnerable than Brutus to the fate of a tragic disintegration. What do we mean when we say that we learn from such an exploration of the moral problems raised by conflicting loyalties, and by the cost of an effective individual response to tyranny? We might mean that we are encouraged by such treatment to lapse into a kind of passivity, eschewing the risk of action in the name of a supposed preservation of our moral innocence. But is this practical lesson the only one that the play teaches? Do we not learn from it something about the human situation, about the perils that beset human action, that lie in wait especially for those who count the cost, and seek to purify at once their motives and their intentions? It is only in action that the secrets of the human heart are revealed, whether we include among those secrets the devices men and women employ rather than confront the abysses of evil, within and without, that open before them.

What sort of facts are these, and what more can we say of the way in which we learn them? We certainly would wish to say that Shakespeare had observed, and also that he had invented; yet we stress his observation to acquit his invention of the taint which affects the term when we use it. If Shakespeare has invented in his play, we are in debt to his invention because it serves the cause of discovery, even conceivably historical discovery; we acknowledge this when we, who have never ourselves been faced with the situation that faced Brutus in the years of Caesar's supremacy, or with that which faced Stauffenberg in those of the Nazi domination of

Germany, claim that we learn from this play concerning what is the case.

Our notion of fact requires liberalisation; but still, of course, it must remain fact. The use of *fact* by such philosophers as Russell and Moore was a relatively technical one. It may indeed be claimed that the radical empiricists' identification of fact with the data of observation seems closer to ordinary everyday usage, which often suggests a close linkage between facts and observation. Yet, as Kant had very clearly shown, and as, of course, Sir Karl Popper had effectively learnt from him, the sense-observation involved in procedures of verification in the experimental and natural sciences possesses an internal complexity which sets a question-mark against its easy invocation by less sophisticated empiricists as a solvent of their question relating to the factual import of what we believe and entertain. But, if in this chapter we have found reasons for liberalising our concepts, both of fact and of observation, we have still to avoid the mistakes characteristic of the thorough-going constructivists.

The temper of the thorough-going 'constructivists' is well represented among some of the present-day theological *avant-garde* and although such writers sometimes seek to render their attitude fashionable by characterising it as 'anti-metaphysical',[5] it is, in fact, much nearer to a radical, if subtly disguised, idealism. Mr Werner Pelz, for instance, boldly affirms that 'faith creates facts', and argues that in as much as faith may be spoken of as a 'matter of decision', this 'decision' must be understood as including the 'willing into existence' that something is the case. For Mr Pelz, and indeed for Dr Paul van Buren, the proposition Christ *was raised from the dead* is identical with the proposition Men *decided to believe that Christ was raised from the dead.* Now the question whether or not Christ *was raised from the dead,* or whether or not any event occurred of such a sort that it satisfied the description *the raising of Christ from the dead* is one of the very greatest intricacy and difficulty. But we are not, I claim, being unduly *simpliste* if we say that it is immediately obvious that when we ask whether or not Christ was raised, we are not asking whether or not men came to believe a certain proposition, irrespective of whether that proposition is true or false, or indeed whether or not that proposition is intelligible or nonsensical. No amount of believing, however passionate (and however we analyse the concept of belief), can bring a dead man from the

[5] I have here particularly in mind an article by Mr Werner Pelz, which appeared in the *Guardian* on Saturday 17 April 1965.

tomb. To some this attitude may suggest a philistine indifference to the heights and depths of the life of faith. Yet if we attend to the phenomenology of faith, it is at least arguable that receptivity is of its very essence, and that it is a response elicited, though not compelled, by external occurrence, and always orientated upon that which lies outside the interior life of the believing subject.

For the moment I wish simply to cite the work of these theologians as an extreme illustration of the temptation to which those who seek to succour a continuing concern with the transcendent are continually prone, namely that of securing its admissibility by releasing it from the need of any submission to the authority of fact. The preceding chapter will have made it plain that I regard those whom I call here constructivists as fully justified in their insistence on the rich complexity of metaphysical, and indeed of religious experience. Yet in my view they are altogether wrong to suppose that this necessary complexity by itself validates the free play of undisciplined inventiveness, or that by the windings of an interior dialectic, we are able to dispense with concern with the factuality of any world with which we have to do.

If we take seriously the question of the significance of the facts we learn from Shakespeare's *Julius Caesar*, we must offer some intelligible account of their factuality, which brings them into relation with those facts we are ready to call facts of observation, in the sense of the more sophisticated empiricists, or with those facts of which the pluralists spoke. If we take seriously the conception of scientific method, implicit in the work of Popper and his disciples, we are certainly allowing far greater weight than the phenomenalists found it easy to concede to the constructive, even speculative, work which must go into the framing of hypotheses. We are here in good company; for Einstein himself has insisted on the inadequacy of the radical empiricists' ignoring of the elements of speculative and constructive, even freely creative, work that must be poured into any effective advance in the territories he has classically made his own.[6]

Yet both Popper and Einstein insist on vulnerability. If we say that the frontiers of fact and observation must be drawn more generously, we have to allow for an analogous extension of the concept of vulnerability. Here indeed lies one of the cruces of our whole enquiry. It may well be, as I would be prepared to argue, that if we

[6] In his essay in the volume on *The Philosophy of Bertrand Russell*, ed. P. A. Schilpp, *Library of living philosophers* (Northwestern University, Evanston, 1950).

take seriously the sort of moral insight contained in such a work as Shakespeare's *Julius Caesar*, we have already advanced beyond the frontiers of, e.g., a thorough-going Benthamite ethical naturalism; *indeed to take such insight seriously is one way of advancing beyond such frontiers; to do it is so to advance.* Yet we serve ourselves very ill, if we suppose that in doing so, we have left the world of fact behind us. How are the facts we learn from such a source related to the facts of observation, stressed with such beneficent, as well as constraining results, by some of those whom we would call empiricist? How, indeed, is the observation on which our knowledge of them, or beliefs concerning them, alike may be thought to rest related to the sort of observation which, for instance, Bentham invoked in defence of the principle of utility, and which is certainly, in Eysenck's view, the only observation warranting us in admitting something as matter of fact? We do not serve discussion of the problem of metaphysics well, if we ever lose sight of the seriousness and manifold character of the case for anti-metaphysics. Still less do we advance the discussion at all if we indulge in the fantasy of supposing that in metaphysics (or indeed in religious belief) we can leave the world of fact behind.

4

Empiricism: a note

In 1815 James Mill boasted in a letter that, given time, he could make the workings of the human mind as plain as the road from Charing Cross to St Paul's Cathedral. It is hardly necessary to add that at that date traffic problems in the Strand were considerably less than they are now! His posthumously published *Analysis of the Human Mind* embodies his attempt to fulfil that undertaking. It is arguably the most ambitious effort made by any single writer standing in the British empiricist tradition to fulfil the aspiration which haunted so many of those adhering to it to be 'the Newton of the moral sciences'. In Mill's two volumes, a full-scale attempt is made to map out the whole universe of human behaviour with laws of association linking impressions and ideas in ways analogous to that in which the worlds of dynamics and astronomy were by consequence of Newton's achievement revealed as satisfying his inverse square law in respect of the manner of the movement of their constituents, one in relation to another.

It is not my intention to discuss in detail James Mill's contribution to the philosophy of mind; a modern student would in fact account it minimal. In fairness to him, however, it may be remarked that his enterprise has its place in the history of empirical psychology in these islands and the struggle of its practitioners at once to establish the methods proper to their investigations and to secure recognition for the latter in universities. Further, the student of Mill's attempted exhaustive exploration of the labyrinths of the human mind will come to understand the target of the poet Coleridge's impassioned protest against a treatment of human consciousness which seemed to him to allow no room for creative, intellectual powers he knew, as a poet, to be in play when exercising that imagination which he painfully sought to distinguish from fancy. The poet enlarged men's understanding both of their natural and their human environment. It was not for nothing that, in his well-known essay on Coleridge, John Stuart Mill accounted him one of the two intellectual master-spirits of the age in which he grew up. Admittedly he set him over against Jeremy Bentham, finding in Bentham rather than his father (and he was surely right) a more rigorous and effective advocate and practitioner of the analytic styles of philosophical activity he thought the characteristic hallmark of the empirical school. His account of Bentham is a more perceptive and illuminating study than the one he attempted of Coleridge. But there is great significance in the way in which he sets the one against the other. One would not be wrong to say that one of the assumptions that Coleridge found most sheerly intolerable in the school in which John Stuart Mill was educated (that of Bentham and his own father) was the assumption concerning the possibility of a definitive mapping of the ways of human consciousness such as James Mill believed to be within his power.

It is characteristic of John Stuart Mill's genius that he leaves the issues between Bentham and Coleridge defined, but unresolved. It is a mixture of insight and irresolution that mars a considerable part of his philosophical writings. He remains in the end the committed empiricist, as for instance in his famous pamphlet on utilitarianism, written after the very different *Essay on Liberty* to salvage as much as he could of the ethical creed in which he was educated. But, as every beginner in moral philosophy learns in the first week of his study, the gaps are left yawning. If such a student is persuaded to return to the earlier and more famous work, he will find Mill pleading with sustained passion the case of the eccentric whose genius may easily be overwhelmed by the pressures of a mass society through philistine denial of the means of expression; such a genius is the 'dissatisfied Socrates' of the later pamphlet. So the student will learn something of the experience that compelled Mill to write as if the doctrine of his earliest schooling could only be salvaged by ill-concealed inconsistency in presentation. It is not for nothing that a moral philosopher may conclude a survey of Mill's writings by saying that no one raises more sharply than he does some of the fundamental questions concealed by the formula *the problem of ethical intuition*, and that without making more contribution towards their solution than may be found through their exhaustive statement.

These brief historical observations are offered by way of introduction to some comments on the metaphysician's preoccupation with the transcendent. We have to ask the question whether such preoccupation is evidence of insight or of obstinacy; we have to ask whether it is fertile and life-giving, or sterile and life-diminishing.

47

Thus this section of my enquiry may be regarded as a contribution to the philosophy of metaphysics, a part of philosophy to which contributions have been made by philosophers as different in situation and temper as Wilhelm Dilthey and Professor John Wisdom. It is also a topic which, in an elusive and tantalising, yet extremely suggestive way, received passionate treatment from the late Professor R. G. Collingwood in his *Essay on Metaphysics* published in the early months of 1940. This work of Collingwood's begins with a curiously distorted criticism of the Aristotelian programme which identified metaphysics with the study of being-*quâ*-being, in which he seems to betray a failure altogether to understand the inwardness of Aristotle's sustained attempt to 'explore the veins and sinews of substance'. But once that aberration is past the work goes on to develop a conception of metaphysics as ultimately a branch of self-knowledge, a conception which indeed underlies a good deal of Collingwood's later work. His *Essay on Metaphysics* appeared in quick succession to the *Autobiography*, published in the previous spring of 1939, a few months before the outbreak of war. In both works, Collingwood had clearly written with what he called the revival of the positivist attack on metaphysics in mind; this though in the *Autobiography* the primary target of his intellectual invective was found in the 'minute philosophers' belonging to the school of the late Professor John Cook-Wilson, whom he arraigned in particular for their studied indifference to questions belonging to the history of philosophy, more particularly to the historical relativity of the philosophical works which they discussed. The open concentration of his energies in the second of these two works on the positivist attack on metaphysics is in some ways paradoxical in that it follows an impatient and curiously unscholarly polemic against the classical Aristotelian view of the metaphysician's task. We must judge that attack impatient and unscholarly not least because, in his *Autobiography*, Collingwood recalls that in his earlier years as a teacher of philosophy in Oxford he had become something of a specialist on Aristotle, lecturing for instance on the *de Anima*. It is this fact, coupled with his avowed respect for rigorous standards of scholarship, that leads one to characterise Collingwood's rejection of the traditional metaphysical style expressed in Aristotle's work as impassioned. It is as if he would not waste time even on the accurate presentation of a philosophical temper which he had agreed with the positivists in rejecting, while at the same time finding in their rejection a more degenerate manifestation of the temper which they criticised.

48

In his Essay on Metaphysics, Collingwood develops in a series of interrelated studies a conception of the metaphysician's task as primarily concerned to lay bare the idées maîtrises which have informed intellectual master-spirits of successive ages. The roll of such masters would include the names of many not usually regarded as philosophers; thus, Galileo, Newton, Clerk-Maxwell, Darwin, Einstein, Dirac, Ranke, Mommsen, even those who, in Collingwood's lifetime, had in his view transformed critical history by their use in the study of the history of Greece of the wealth of archaeological material suddenly available; for instance, Alan Blakeway and Theodore Wade-Gery would have their place upon it. It was the task of the philosopher to enable his contemporaries to achieve self-conscious awareness of the presuppositions which informed the most advanced investigation of the world at the time at which they lived. In the studies in the history of philosophy included in this work on metaphysics, Collingwood illustrates this thesis by reference to the theology of the so-called 'Athanasian Creed', on the one hand, and Kant's 'Analytic of Principles' on the other. One might say that a part of his thesis represents a brilliant generalisation of the frequently canvassed suggestion that Kant in his First Critique is concerned, whether he knows it or not, to vindicate the fundamental laws of Newtonian physics as inviolable principles involved in the very possibility of objective awareness of the world about us. Collingwood writes under the clear conviction that with the advent of historical self-consciousness we are able both to evaluate the work of previous metaphysicians, for instance the Kant of the 'Analytic', and presumably continue their tradition by a new move in metaphysical philosophising, in which we articulate the presuppositions not simply of a supposed contemporary world view but of an understanding of the world that must reckon with a new awareness of the historical relativity of all such views. Of so significant a mutation of consciousness, Collingwood gives no detailed positive account, only suggesting both in this work and in his posthumously published work on history (incorporating much material of an earlier date than the works he published in 1939 and 1940) that the enterprise is essential to an authentic self-knowledge and response to the demands of contemporary life.

Collingwood's programme is arguably capable of uses to which he himself would have been unwilling to put it. This especially if the student complements it by reference to Dilthey's illuminating classification and analysis of fundamentally divergent metaphysical styles.

It is with such an extension of Collingwood's method that the present chapter of this work is concerned. Indeed, the introductory remarks on John Stuart Mill's relations to his father's intellectual ambition, and its significance for the inconsistencies in his own work may be recognised as the beginning of just such an essay. Mill's commitment was fundamentally empirical, and it is from the empiricist commitment that he moved in the ways in which he did towards a painfully achieved and hardly defended recognition of its limitations. It is a mark of such commitment to manifest a kind of standing impatience with the sort of preoccupation with the transcendent that in this work has been judged a common mark of the metaphysician. Since the work of the Vienna Circle initiated by Professor Moritz Schlick's revival of the traditions of Ernst Mach and his incorporation into them of insights extracted from Russell's logic and Wittgenstein's earlier writing, the empiricist is usually identified by adherence to some form of verification principle, even by a generalised, continuing attachment to a phenomenalist programme. By a generalised attachment I mean one that does not narrowly restrict the programme to one of the effective reduction of statements concerning material objects to sets of statements concerning actual and possible sense-contents, but rather conceives its general policy as largely akin to that of the so-called 'descriptive theory of science'. It is a commitment to seek as far as possible the means whereby statements relating, e.g., to the supposedly unobservable entities in physical theory may be converted into statements somehow referring to what man may actually see, hear, touch, smell, taste. The absurdity of the 'descriptive theory' is now sufficiently obvious for the programme to require a vastly more sophisticated formulation than it received when in the early years of the Vienna Circle it seemed as if the philosopher's task could be identified with the generalisation of the sort of critical argument that had enabled Mach to eliminate the notion of an ether posited simply as a medium of undulation, and to criticise with devastating insight the thesis of absolute motion. It is a common-place to insist that the phenomenalist programme has broken down; (indeed of course in the middle thirties its collapse was already evident in the opting of Otto Neurath and Rudolph Carnap for a programme of logical materialism in preference to the more conventional empiricism of Moritz Schlick). Yet, the impulse behind the phenomenalist programme remains, and with its collapse one is perhaps able more effectively to extract its underlying force in a commitment to actual observation as the supreme authority in controversy concerning matter of fact. It was in 1934 that Dr Karl Popper published his very influential *Logik der Forschung*, a work in which the influence of Kant's appraisal of experimental method is strong and in which sharp criticism is offered of traditional empiricist emphasis, for instance on the supreme significance of allegedly immediate experience and inductive arguments taking the records of such experience as its starting-point. Popper's work remains influential in ways in which the earlier, more radical work of the Vienna School does not. Yet historically it emerges as a critical comment on the immense self-confidence of that school in its earliest years and the force with which it formulated the principle of a thorough-going empiricist commitment. And this it had done initially in part by the negative challenge it issued to any claim, for instance, to mysterious insight into allegedly universal and necessary principles defended by such phenomenologists as Max Scheler as beyond critical scrutiny.

No one concerned with the problem of metaphysics who felt the sharp interrogation of the positivist challenge can ever forget the experience – this though the many inadequacies of the positivist outlook are now glaringly obvious. Where the philosopher of science is concerned, Popper's work has borne the test of time in ways in which the more confident essays of those whom he criticised have tended to date. Yet his insistence that no hypothesis has the right to be called scientific which is not vulnerable in principle to observational refutation is genetically continuous with the kind of reductionist programme which it sought constructively to criticise. It embodies in fact a more disciplined variant of the earlier thesis; or one might say that in Popper's own work and the work that has followed from it, the empiricist tradition has been 'de-mythologised'. To grasp that tradition, however, in its dynamic force, one may do worse than study its more extreme manifestations. For there one finds in its reassertion in the thirties, a new and remarkably powerful continuation of the sort of tradition represented in the eighteenth century by the writers of the French Encyclopedia. Indeed it was the men of the Vienna Circle who helped to launch the project of an 'encyclopaedia of unified science', a work which the outbreak of the Second World War brought to an end but which included in its first published fascicules some work of considerable value. One must not forget that this revival of a very powerful tradition of European thought took place against the background of the period between the wars when very different attitudes were encouraged and indeed established for long periods in positions of hardly challengeable political power. One could even say that its extremity and extravagance owed something to the fact that historically it belonged to a world of extremes.

If therefore we are to ask the question whether preoccupation with the transcendent is a mark of intellectual insight or of obstinacy, a source of life-enhancement or something sterilising and deadly, one does well to recall something of the outlook of those who, in the philosophical accents of the thirties, cried, 'Ecrasez l'infâme.' Intellectually it may well be said that the metaphysician imprisons himself in obsession with questions which he cannot hope to answer. Indeed, in the very framing of these questions he may expect to find that he has violated the conditions of intelligibility, indulging in a totally indefensible confusion of different sorts of discourse in order to set himself problems that admit as little of statement as they do of solution. It is as if he moves beyond the frontiers of a world in which questions may be asked and answered or at least, if not answered, left open questions, the circumstances that render them unanswerable being clearly specified. One does not need to know much concerning developments in such fields as radio-astronomy and electron-microscopy to see that in the years before the vast technological advances on which the work of radio-astronomers and those who for various purposes use electron-microscopy, depend, the sorts of questions to which answers may now be found were in fact unanswerable; but if anyone had asked them, he could only have been accused of folly, hardly blamed for talking nonsense – this though, where the map of the universe in time as well as in space is concerned, the work of the radio-astronomer may well effect transformations altogether undreamt in previous ages. But what the techniques involved in electron-microscopy and radio-astronomy have made possible is the putting of hypotheses to precisely formulable relevant tests. Are there any tests relevant to the claims that men may make about that which must by definition lie altogether beyond the reach of possible observation? Is the very conception of such a dimension of being admissible? Or is the attempt to conceive it not rather a deflection of energies from the sorts of enquiry that may in fact enlarge men's understanding both of their world and of themselves? It is with such questions as these that this whole work is concerned. Accordingly it is prudent at this stage in the argument to recall some aspects of the positivist polemic against metaphysical preoccupation to ensure the clearest possible statement of the problems.

5

Ethics and metaphysics

This chapter is concerned with Kant's doctrine of the primacy of practical reason, a topic to which I have already alluded in chapter 3 of this work. In Butler's fifteenth sermon in the Rolls Chapel, a doctrine of the primacy of practical reason is stated which bears certain very interesting resemblances to Kant's, but which is also significantly different from it. 'Creation', Butler writes, 'is obviously and entirely out of our depth, and beyond the extent of our utmost search.'

Here Butler writes in frankly agnostic style, and we could continue his argument to the point of saying that for him the employment of the concept *creatio de nihilo*, once we have purged its use of anthropomorphic overtones and undertones, plunges us into something akin to complete aphasia. Yet Butler continues that it is as certain that God made the world, as it is certain that effects must have a cause. He is quite confident of our warrant to employ the category of causality in attaching the world to its ultimate origin. No hesitation attends his extrapolation of the concept, however opaque the yield of our doing so to our understanding. Yet he also insists that it is no more than effects that the most knowing are acquainted with; for as to causes, they are entirely in the dark, even as the most ignorant. Butler here is repeating, in different form, his conviction that the manner of the divine causality is altogether opaque to us; that while we can trace patterns of order in the tapestry of the universe, the creative and sustaining act which brought into being at once that tapestry and its manifold design, is wholly obscure to us. He does not, surprisingly enough, draw the obvious conclusion that even to use the term 'causality' in respect of such an act is to employ the concept in ways so totally unrelated to its familiar use that we cannot know what we are about in its employment here. It is as if Butler is prepared, almost without argument, to defend a quite unsophisticated use of the concept of causality in respect of the transcendent, at once to make confession of a conviction and to advertise an insoluble problem. The universe has a first cause; of that we may be confident, though we neither know what we mean when we affirm such a derivation, nor enjoy any sort of familiarity with that from which the world is derived nor understand the primacy we attribute to this cause. He goes on to argue that this deficiency need not disturb us; indeed, it has a genuinely therapeutic value, provided we can lay to heart its lessons.

Butler insists vehemently in this sermon that we do not have to wait upon cosmological discovery (and it is possibly empirical cosmological discovery that he here intends), to acknowledge the supreme authority of that conscience with whose nature and role the sermons have been so largely concerned. Conscience abides, and we must acknowledge its claim upon us; even if much concerning the world to which we belong is hidden from us, this obscurity must not for one moment deter us from obeying its voice. His argument recalls the Socratic retreat from cosmological speculation. The authority of the moral consciousness (differently conceived by Butler) is exalted and made totally independent of any general insight, however won, concerning the way in which things are. We do not need to wait till the secrets of heaven and earth are known to us to recognise the peremptory authority of the moral order.

Much of this reads like an unsophisticated version of Kant's argument. Yet not in all respects; for Kant could never have been naive enough epistemologically to write that it is as certain that God made the world as that effects must have causes. Kant's doctrine of the primacy of practical reason was a much more radical one than Butler's. Both philosophers can rightly be characterised as metaphysical agnostics; but Kant's agnosticism is much more formally grounded, and rigorously argued, than Butler's, extending to depths which the bishop does not reach. Its limitations are well illustrated by this confident, almost offhand, assumption of the category of causality as validly used in divinis. Whatever else may be said on the subject of Kant's treatment of metaphysics, few could dispute the claim that he submits most, if not all, forms of the causal argument for the existence of God to most searching criticism. This he is able to do because a renewed understanding of the significance and role of the notion of causality is central to the programme of his descriptive metaphysics. As we have suggested, and as we must emphasise again, he believes he has established its indispensability, properly understood, to the very possibility of objects of experience. But because it is significant only in so far as it is thus shown to be indispensable, its employment in the attempt to relate that objective world to its supposed ultimate origin is a gross violation of its proper sense. In attempting to use the notion to broach the very outskirts of the transcendent, we are guilty of a logical offence; to speak crudely, we are trying to jump out of our cognitive skins.

Therefore Kant's agnosticism (if we avert attention for a moment from what Professor Strawson refers to as his 'metaphysics of transcendental idealism'[1]), is unqualified by any such concession as Butler makes to traditional metaphysics. There is, indeed, in Butler's language an echo of the well-known remark of St Thomas Aquinas: 'Of God we know that he is, what he is not, and what relation everything else has to him.' Here (whatever we may say of other passages in his writings), Thomas allows the use of the concept of causality, as it were, to launch our thoughts towards the deeps of the divine. He is agnostic, sophisticatedly so; but his agnosticism is qualified, even as Butler's is, whereas Kant would seem to have established a veto on every attempt to give sense to the ways in which we conceive the relation of the familiar to the transcendent, even (and this is crucial) to the bare statement that such ontological derivation obtains.[2]

Kant's doctrine of the primacy of practical reason remains an almost classical expression of one approach to the problem of metaphysics; I mean the approach which sees the metaphysical as something lying beyond the frontiers of intelligible descriptive discourse, yet as something that *presses* on us with a directness and immediacy which requires no argument to convince us of its reality.[3] Yet even to use the language of reality here is to be involved in a violation of the limitation which Kant has established in his doctrine of objectivity concepts. Its use is the point at which the rigorous prohibition of Kant's agnostic programme is defined, and we find ourselves plunging desperately to make sense of a use of language which is at one and the same moment demanded by the moral experience *which indeed it makes possible*, and ruled out as illegitimate by Kant's own critical analysis of the conditions of objectivity. Of course, Kant seeks to void ethical language of descriptive referential import. Its proper mood is imperative, not indicative; it speaks always of the world of *Sollen* in the context of action. Yet to present oneself with

[1] In his book on Kant, *The Bounds of Sense* (Methuen, 1966).
[2] See the note appended to the end of this chapter on Kant's treatment of the theistic proofs.
[3] It is the analysis of this pressure that constitutes the crux of this book.

a categorical imperative is indirectly to make assertion concerning the stuff of which we are made, to present, indeed, ourselves to ourselves in a way which most certainly transcends the frontiers of the empirically discernible, but which, at the same time, we find ourselves compelled to regard as supremely and ultimately significant.[4]

Although Kant, as we have seen, is one of the most illuminating critics of the project of transcendent metaphysics, his own doctrine of the primacy of practical reason is an almost classical expression of a particular approach to the problem of metaphysics. Those who favour his approach see 'the metaphysical' as something lying outside the frontiers of intelligible discourse. It is, indeed, an approach also clearly discernible in Wittgenstein's *Tractatus*, a work in which Professor Erik Stenius has found fascinating resemblances to Kant.[5] Yet Kant can, in an important sense, be described as a speculative metaphysician, and in his very valuable study of the *Critique of Pure Reason*, Professor Strawson has accused him of a gross violation of his own principles, in his development of a 'metaphysics of transcendental idealism'. Yet the element in the *Critique* on which Strawson fastens in this section of his study, is in a measure propaedeutic to Kant's doctrine of the primacy of practical reason; it provides the context within which this primacy is to be understood and is, indeed, much more clearly integrated with his programme of descriptive metaphysics as part of a total propaedeutic study than Strawson allows.

Kant's whole enterprise is suffused by his sense of that which lies outside the frontiers of intelligible discourse. These frontiers he has drawn, and drawn in such a way that whereas a man may, indeed must, significantly speak of his tiredness on a particular afternoon as having a cause, or a sudden explosion as having a cause, or indeed of any event whatever as having a cause, he cannot speak of events as such, that is the total furniture of the time-order as having a cause.

---

[4] One notes here three discriminable elements: (a) the epistemological insistence on what is in no sense empirically discernible; (b) the moral insistence on that which is regarded as of highest value; (c) what one can call by extremely irregular usage, claim to ontological ultimacy. (The use of 'ontological' in this note is a besetting problem in this book.) Here we deal with a range of facts irreducibly distinct from every other, surpassing all others in ontological dignity. The grounds on which we predicate such dignity of them remain obscure; the very notion of the act of predication itself is a logical outrage, which we do not banish by insisting that its context is an exigency of practical life, not an expression of the cultivated detachment of theoretical enquiry.

[5] Erik Stenius, *Wittgenstein's Tractatus* (Blackwell, 1960).

It is quite illegitimate to extrapolate the notion of cause, indispensable to the possibility of objective description, outside the context which such description constitutes. Yet Kant is aware that outside these limits there lies what, for him, is supremely significant in human life; of course, to speak in these terms is to use spatial and temporal imagery, and to tempt the student to represent to himself a relationship which Kant insists, by strenuous and tortuous argument, is in principle incapable of representation. So he goes a long way beyond opinions expressed almost in slapdash manner by Butler in his sermon on the ignorance of man. The latter's moral philosophy was presented in the form of sermons, and they were the sermons of a man for whom the proposition *God exists* was undoubtedly true. He sought to persuade his hearers that it was more important that they should sort out and know their own motives, and take measure of the complex, human stuff of which they were made, than that they should exhaust themselves in fruitless speculation concerning the modes and manner of transcendent being, and the arcana of the relations in which the detail of the world's manifold handiwork stood to God's all-originating and all-sustaining causality. Our true worship lay in obedience to the prescriptions of our conscience. Yet God's existence was, for all that, presupposed by Butler's whole thought, imposing on him that disciplined attention to the complex detail of our actual human nature, which is one of his greatest qualities as a moralist, whereas Kant, although in the end a theist, is of a different temper. His God does not enter into the texture of his exposition; he is not an omnipresent first cause, whose sovereign purpose can be discerned in the minute complexities of our actual nature. Rather he lies altogether beyond the frontiers of intelligible referential and descriptive statement. We are all the time thrust (one needs a word which will be innocent of misleading cognitive import) outside those frontiers, precipitated beyond them by a moral experience on whose formal unity, in the most diverse human situations, Kant insists.

No modern philosopher raises more acutely than Kant, the problem of the representation of the unrepresentable, the problem of assuming to the full the disciplines of *theologia negativa*, and then, as it were, seeking to escape from them. So far in this chapter I have been concerned to emphasise the constricting force of these disciplines, the manner in which they seem to crib, cabin and confine our eagerness to thrust beyond the limits of the intelligible. Yet, there is another side to the matter. It is precisely this sense of the uncontrollable quality of the ultimate which enables Kant to assign to the ontologically intractable reality (to use a word which Kant's own argument in the *Critique of Pure Reason* might justifiably be thought to prohibit) of human freedom the ultimacy which he believes to belong to it.

No moralist took human freedom more seriously than Kant. What was it for a human being to be morally free? When we say that we are morally free, according to Kant, we regard ourselves as the authors of what we do; we are, in fact, the first causes of what we bring into being. Here again we encounter the central chasm in Kant's thinking, that attempted combination of a well-grounded rejection of the whole idiom of first causality, with the demand that we reintroduce the notion in the novel context of our self-characterisation as moral beings. If 'ought implies can', and this proposition is certainly fundamental to Kant's ethics, then we must be the authors of that which we are morally bound to bring into being. The idiom for the modern reader seems suffused with an unhealthy desire that what we do should be laid at our door; the imagery it evokes is that of an assize court in which the defendant must always be found fit to plead. Yet one can, in a measure, rescue this emphasis from these misleading and unpalatable associations, by speaking more of human creativity and less of human accountability. Are men and women, or are they not, originators – originators not only of, for instance, works of art and literature, but also of what is sometimes called, by use of a not unimpressive analogy, the poems of their own lives? Suppose we let our attention wander across the ages, and remember the figures of Socrates, Francis of Assisi, Abraham Lincoln, Schweitzer; one could continue indefinitely, and without sentimental illusion concerning the flaws that, in differing ways, mar these individuals. Certainly we must not commit ourselves to any romantic concept of moral genius; these men, all of them, belonged to historical contexts and environments, which at once nourished and limited their responses. Yet we regard them all as men who, in spite of their faults, have, in very different ways, enlarged our concept of what it is to be a human being; and this is an enlargement of which they are themselves regarded as the effective agents, through what they have made of the hardly tractable material of their inheritance. Kant admittedly draws the difficult conclusion that, in them all, their moral goodness was formally one, that what we mean by speaking of them as morally good was *mutatis omnibus mutandis* the same in all of them, in that, from the confused wholes of their moral obedience, we could extract and reveal as always present a common formal pattern. Yet, even if we have to modify Kant's doctrine substantially here, we cannot gainsay the importance of his emphasis that in such men we have to reckon with a kind of origination for which we claim ultimacy, an ultimacy that is inconceivable in the sense that the manner in which it transcends the familiar world is impatient of any sort of representation.

It belongs to Kant's whole doctrine of the primacy of practical reason to insist that freedom is a sort of first causality, to which we can, *within the context of the moral life*, assign significance. As soon as we have thus restricted the designate of the term 'first cause' and, in effect, vetoed any attempt to find the referent of the notion in the realm of being, we come to see that our understanding of the human situation is advanced and deepened. We cannot, Kant seems to say, have it both ways. If a man affirms that there is a first cause of all that is, and attends to what he says, then the lives of individual men and women, as much as anything else, depend asymmetrically upon this unitary, all-determining, all-originating being. We can accuse Kant of a lack here of metaphysical subtlety, of his grasp of the relation of secondary to primary causality; but he compensates with the force by which he brings home the contradiction between the monistic habit of mind, which would seek to embrace, within a single scheme, all time and all existence, and that habit of mind which takes seriously the actuality of human freedom. For Kant, ontological conception of a transcendent first cause expelled freedom from the position of ultimacy he claimed that it must possess. The universe of the speculative metaphysician is a closed universe; whereas the universe of moral agents must be an open one.

There is a kind of tormenting complexity in Kant's argument. He has seen a whole lot of things at once. For instance, he has seen that the libertarian, and Kant is beyond question a libertarian, however qualified his attitude to 'freedom of open possibilities', is bound to be a metaphysical agnostic, in the sense of refusing to allow that we can achieve a vantage-point from which to see things as they are, as necessarily working together for fulfilment of a single comprehensive purpose, justifying itself and all else in terms of itself. The hostility to the synoptic impulse of the metaphysician is deeply engrained in Kant; it must never be forgotten that for him it was often the Leibnizian tradition which provided the very paradigm of metaphysical achievement, and in his work, which in part at least made possible a deepened understanding of the metaphysical impulse, it was against the traditions of the Leibnizian schools that he was reacting. We may regret the deficiencies of his immediate philosophical inheritance; yet we must be glad that through his sustained criticism of the 'principle of sufficient reason' (the keystone of the arch of the tradition which he rejected), he presented the problem of metaphysics with a new depth, revealing the paradox that a proper ethical seriousness makes a man at once on edge in the presence of a self-confident naturalism or seemingly confining empiricist criticism, and yet, at the same time, pulls him away from the confident synopsis of the master of speculation. The project of a survey of all time and all existence is at once intellectually vacuous, and morally dangerous; and in so far as it is the latter, it is a projected distortion of what is often its fundamental impulse. If, by systematic construction, we give the suitable shape of a finished doctrine to our discontent with naturalism, we destroy the deepest foundations of that discontent itself. We have to come to admit an advancement of our moral understanding, through the banishment from the world as critically inadmissible of the theoretical all-embracing.

And yet, of course, we are in very great difficulties. How can we attach any sense whatsoever to the claim that we are sometimes the first causes of what we do? It is certainly Kant's conviction that morally free action cannot be recognised as an item in the series of events which make up the history of the world. Certainly we are tempted to speak of such actions as breaking natural continuities; but this is mythology; for the continuity of the world's processes is an inescapable assumption of their successful study. The supposed violations of these continuities which we encounter inescapably demand their own integration within some sort of comprehensible series. It is not of such relative violations that we speak when we refer to free action, but to an absolute novelty, something whose notion we have only to formulate to find it incapable of representation.

For any event which happens, and our actions are as much events in their way as hurricanes, earthquakes, attacks of gastro-enteritis, hallucinations, the cooling of the earth's surface, the disappearance of the great prehistoric monsters – I could go on at random – there is another event such that an instance of an event of the one sort is (for Kant) also necessarily an instance of an event of the other. An act of self-sacrifice is rooted in an occurrent desire on the agent's part to punish himself.

For Kant there is in any actual causal transaction an elusive necessity; such a process was not for him reducible simply to an instance of regularity. Yet a great deal of what is most important in his argument needs no more than a causality analysed in terms of the unbroken co-variation of the characteristics of individual events standing in determinate spatio-temporal relations, one to another. The assumption of such regularity is for Kant a condition of the very possibility of objectively referential description, in particular the recognition of a single, public, temporal direction, but also, indeed, the very distinction between objectively real and unreal. It is because his transcendental proof of the so-called principle of causality finds that principle indispensable to the positing of a single trans-subjective, temporal direction, that Kant approaches the intensely difficult question of the relation of the moral order to the natural world by insisting that the actions belonging to the former are timeless. This suggestion is so flamboyantly paradoxical as to be virtually a non-sense, especially when one recalls the extent to which Kant's ethics emphasise, for instance, the interior moral self-discipline of the individual, a process hardly in any sense conceivable, except as one demanding periods of time for its perfection. 'Take no thought of reaping, only of proper sowing.' These words of T. S. Eliot capture an important aspect of the Kantian *Gesinnungsethik*. Yet can we attach any sense whatsoever to a non-temporal sowing? Initially, by stressing the alleged timelessness of moral actions, Kant would seem to wish to advertise simply their apartness from the objective world, even by implication to insist on the sheer equivocity of sense, in using the term 'cause' in respect of the cause of an event in time (for instance, the cause of a sudden bang outside the room where I am presently writing), and in respect of an absolutely first cause. The way in which a man regards himself when, in practical life, he assumes his own primary causality, has nothing in common with the causality he assumes as fundamental to the continuity of the natural world to which he belongs.

Of course, we have to recall another aspect of Kant's doctrine here, viz. his treatment of space and time as genetically forms of outer and inner sense, as modes of characteristically human experience in con-tradistinction from divine or absolute awareness. Again, where that awareness is concerned, we must (as we have already seen) be altogether agnostic. Yet as soon as we recall the subjectivity of space and time (or that element of it on which we have fastened), we loosen our sense of the almost all-enveloping embrace of these forms so inescapably pervasive to our experience, yet so intimately expressive of our characteristically human subjectivity.

Kant's thought is a fascinating and maddening amalgam of disparate elements held together by a man who eschews the intellectual escape-route of analogy, preferring to set down over against each other, as it were, the four pieces of an intellectual puzzle.

1. There is a sharp sense of the very depth with which the assumption of lawful regularity lies at the foundation of objective experience in general, and awareness of a unitary time-order possessing linear direction in particular.

2. There is his recognition that, while time remains the most pervasive form of characteristically human experience, apart from which we can attach no meaning to the idea of such experience and to the problems involved in its articulation (the problems to whose solution 'objectivity-concepts' or categories are indispensable) yet it is of characteristically *human* intellectual experience that time is the form.

3. There is a haunting sense that the notion of the transcendent, and the relation of the transcendent to the familiar, breaks in upon us at the level of practical life, and that in choice, decision, action etc., we are projected into commerce with the ultimate, even if our relation to it resists altogether intelligible representation.

4. There is, further, Kant's conviction that if, indeed, it is at the level of practical life that we enjoy our commerce with the ultimate, then the axis of our human dignity is our freedom. The agnosticism which issues from his criticism of transcendent metaphysics as a theoretical enquiry, while seeming to condemn him to a kind of total aphasia concerning the ultimate, yet, at the same time enables him to assign to freedom its supreme significance and irreducible import.

It is by paradoxical assertion that moral action is timeless, that these four insights (if so they may be characterised) are held together. We can understand how such characterisation renders the status of moral action altogether inconceivable. We can understand, also, how it sets the causality involved in such action apart from that which we find indispensable to intelligible description of matters of fact; so the practical is prised apart from the theoretical. Further, the flamboyant paradox of the assertion suggests that in the traditional metaphysical triad of God, freedom, and immortality, speculative concern with the first and third may cut short too quickly attention to the arcana of the second, especially when the first – God – is approached in Leibnizian terms suggesting (if only the antinomous elements in the conception can be mastered), a universe as little fitted to be a home for free action as that of Laplace himself.

It is fundamental to Kant's whole argument that if we seek to deepen our self-consciousness concerning our moral commitment as human beings, we must avert from the sort of understanding that comes by way of causal explanation, its refinements, its analogues, its suggested extrapolations. Most certainly we can and should seek to understand ourselves, as much as our natural environment, by the aid of such explanatory procedures. There is nothing in Kant suggestive of any hostility to empirical psychological and sociological investigation; indeed, there is much in him which would find a frankly behaviourist temper congenial. On the central epistemological topic of the relation of self-knowledge to knowledge of the external world, he wrote and argued with an intense concentration remarkable even for him. If he is often carelessly branded as an idealist, he spent a great deal of energy in establishing the extent to which self-understanding was parasitic upon knowledge of the world about us. Yet, outside the scope of such understanding there lay the world of morality. Indeed, the irreducibility, the ultimacy, the dignity of that world assumed sharper and clearer definition through contrast with the growing yield of factual investigation, where self-knowledge was concerned. It is a world which cannot be represented, a world which, indeed, we come to acknowledge for what it is, only when we recognise that it cannot be represented.

Yet how can we in any sense acknowledge its reality without the beginnings of an attempt at representation? The insistence that it is timeless may be thought to stand as a final veto on any attempt to characterise it; yet the very effort to advance, even by affirming its reality, involves us in the application of categories to things in themselves. To use less loaded Kantian language, we employ the notion of existence, in a way that defies our every effort to relate what we are doing in its application here to other formally acceptable examples of a similar procedure. So our separation of the realm of nature from the realm of freedom involves us in such equivocation, in the very characterisation of the two as realms, that we must admit a complete ignorance in what it is that we are achieving by thus referring to the two. If we go further, and say we belong to both realms, we are in danger, by our intellectual indulgence in use even of that rarefied metaphor, of supposing that in however vague and elusive a way, the patterns of the natural realm and the moral realm correspond. Yet the matter cannot rest there; for we know that we ourselves belong to both realms, and this quite simply because we are ourselves agents whose actions are also objects for our understanding, in whose biographies causal continuities can clearly be traced, whose behaviour is in a measure not only predictable in principle, but predictable in practice. It is only, therefore, when we recognise the inherent limitations of that understanding's operation that we can school ourselves to the acknowledgement of that which lies outside its scope. Yet, in the end we face the question how we are to say anything of that which lies outside those limits, without using those very concepts which we have restricted to use within the limits of experience, *partly to establish room for the claim upon us of that which we say lies altogether outside that experience.* The contradiction there is inescapable. It is focussed in the fact that, for Kant, human beings as moral agents are the first causes of their actions and that so to characterise their relation to those actions is to use the word 'cause' in a way that bears no representable or traceable relation to its uses when we speak of the causes of Jones' neurosis, my present cold in the head, earthquakes and unexpectedly high tides, etc. Primary causality has been wrenched apart from the causality of nature by the extravagance of speaking of the former as timeless. But what, if anything, does that achieve except to advertise that what is most fundamental is beyond the reach of representation? Yet without the effort at representation, what is left but aphasia?

So much of Kant's speculative metaphysical philosophy is a kind of play on the theme of the relation of the two worlds of nature and of morality. In Kant nature is the by-us-observable world. If we use the term 'world' to refer to nature, and then go on to speak of the 'world' of morality, we do not know what we say. So although in Kant there is much which we can only call speculative metaphysics, it is the speculative metaphysics of a philosopher who had ruled out such an enterprise as impossible, who indeed developed a descriptive metaphysics, and an analysis of conceptual thinking which was intended to indicate precisely why such an enterprise must be frustrated.

Yet, in the second two *Critique's*, and in his *Opuscula*, the theme of the two worlds is continually in play. One could sum the matter up by saying that the agnosticism which he believed secured the reality of the freedom (whatever the word 'reality' means in this context) proved more than flesh and blood could stand. For his understanding of human morality (formalist and restricted though we may call it), demanded an individual who belonged to both realms at once. Those aspects of the doctrine of the *Grundlegung* which many readers find most uncongenial are unintelligible unless we suppose an individual poised between the conflicting claims upon his allegiance of individual and collective purposes, on the one side, and of the 'realms of ends' on the other. It is the latter's transcendent authority which, in Kant's view, the individual must try to affirm in the varied relativities of actual life. Moreover, Kant was too realistic in his moral understanding not to attend to the ineradicable involvement of human individuals in the changes and chances of their natural environment, which is by no means always under their control, nor likely to become so in any foreseeable future. Again, practical political effort is weakened if we do not possess some assurances of a purpose outside ourselves, which bends even our conflicting egoisms to service of a morally acceptable end. Thus, he argues, in his pamphlet on *Perpetual Peace* that we should allow more weight to the pessimism of Hobbes than to the relative optimism of Locke; yet we need not be dismayed by this concession. So he encourages his readers to entertain the 'idea of progress', as an 'as if', calculated to encourage us in fidelity to the claims of the moral universe. But it is an 'idea of progress' sharply differentiated through this transformation of its status from that characteristic of the *Aufklärung*,[6] whose conceptions here, as often, Kant sought to deepen in his own highly individual way.

So the agnosticism which is the very foundation of his vindication of the reality of freedom is complemented by a series of 'as if's'. These 'as if's' are not all of the same pattern. And here we should recall not only his longer works, but also his remarkable essay on the philosophy of religion, and the curious fragment (for it is no more) on the 'last things'. We cannot understand what it is to act freely in the way in which we can understand what it is, e.g., to act without visible constraint, whether in the shape of prison bondage, or compulsive neurosis. If we say that we are free, when we mean that we are not at present in jail, nor slaves of uncontrollable destructive urges, we may say that which is empirically true, and which is certainly important; but such freedom is most certainly not emancipation from causal law. Our behaviour remains, in principle, causally intelligible, whether we are in prison or out of it; whether we are in need of psychiatric care or chemotherapy or not. A man who no longer finds himself at the beck and call of prison officers, and subject to a drab routine, has still to allow that his actions are, in a measure, predictable. From a knowledge of what we have been

[6] We should never forget the depth of Kant's debt in ethics to Rousseau.

and are, our reaction to sudden emergency may be forecast. Assuredly this is more a matter of intelligible continuity than bondage; yet it is very far removed from that first causality, in virtue of which we say that we are the initiators of what we do. We can form no picture of such self-hood, imagine no content for such causality; yet it is Kant's claim that we can see its bare possibility. So in his phrase reason is destroyed to make room for rational faith.

Yet again we ask how we are to give flesh and blood to this conviction. Suppose we use a much over-worked term, and speak of the reality of the moral universe as a myth; we then have to ask what forms this mythology is to assume, and how these forms are to be understood. For Kant, moral discovery, in the sense of the recognition of ourselves as moral beings, is something utterly fundamental. If philosophy has any claim to practical import, that claim would seem to reside in part, for him, in the way in which it enables us to make this discovery. We do not invent our moral nature (to invoke again the opposition of discovery and invention). Rather it is something which we disclose to ourselves. The process of philosophising, recapitulated and impressionistically presented here, issues in discovery in something which we have to accept. Here Kant and Butler are in agreement. Even as, for the latter, the authority of conscience is something thrust upon us, so for Kant the unconditional character of moral obligation is an inescapable, the most inescapable, feature of our human situation. Yet it is a discovery presented through tortuous and strenuous argument, whose structure torments the reader; for it includes at its centre the recognition that what we have discovered we can neither represent nor, indeed, rest in recognition of its unrepresentability. To do the latter is to condemn ourselves to an aphasia Kant was certainly not prepared to impose upon himself.

Recently I have introduced the term 'as if', and in Kant's later writing there is much that can be gathered under this rubric. The possibility of moral discovery in the fundamental scale of the disclosure of ourselves to ourselves as moral beings, is presented by Kant as something at once akin to, yet different from, traditional metaphysical discourse. It is subordinate to the purposes for which we use it, significant in relation to them, and criticisable by the reference to the effectiveness or non-effectiveness of its service; and these purposes may be summed up as the achievement of a purchasehold on the ultimacy and irreducibility of our moral dignity. But what we speak of in terms of 'as if', is less itself a matter of discovery than the wide-ranging complex conditions of the possibility of such discovery. We are concerned with the conditions of self-discovery, and it may be of fidelity to the self so discovered. What emerges out of our study of Kant's work may at first seem to be regarded as an attempted detachment of speculative metaphysics from ontology, at least in the Aristotelian sense. Yet this would be an over-simplification in that Kant cannot, in the end, be judged indifferent to the project of ontological enquiry. Rather, he comes very near identifying speculative metaphysics with the articulation of its problem or, rather, converting the articulation of the problem into something whose significance can only be seen in the relation to the practical life, but whose near-indispensability for the proper orientation of that life can be established.

I say near-indispensability; this character of the 'as if' should be sharply distinguished from the indispensability of Kant's objectivity-concepts. It does not admit of anything remotely akin to 'transcendental deduction'; its various expressions have their origin in a diversity of sources; they are much looser in texture, vindicated by their power to suggest, rather than by more compulsive proof. The articulation of the problem of metaphysics itself is, however, a special case. It is partly for this reason that it demands an extended study, almost as if it were the universal form unifying together the disparate, inevitably fragmentary, yet indispensable essays through which it achieves its most effective expression.

In Kant's ethics, no single conception is more important than that of the realm of ends. It is a grave mistake to forget, however, that this concept is an abstraction from one formulation of the supreme principle of morality. In the beginning is the categorical imperative, and it is within that imperative that the concept of the realm of things is significant. It is a crude mistake to treat it as a geographical or sociological or political concept. There is no realm of ends; rather, all the time we acknowledge its sovereignty in our relations with our fellows, and this when these relations are inevitably and properly functional in character. We cannot make a model of what it is to treat human nature as an end, and not merely as a means, as if we could represent to ourselves in the concrete, the realisation of this imperative. We cannot make such a model because the diversity of human relationships is indefinite, and whether we confess our failures in public, or in private, in fulfilment of the responsibilities of public office, or in the haphazard contexts of everyday life, we still acknowledge its sovereignty. Yet, although we cannot design a blueprint for the achievement of such a relation, it is interesting we can invoke manifold resources of imagery to convey to ourselves the kind of thing to which we are bound. Kant notoriously deprecated examples as the 'go-cart of the understanding'. But here we have to do with more than examples; almost it is with projections of the inwardness of the moral imperative on to the screen of observable fact.

But to what extent do such images advance our insight into what morality is? Here Kant writes uncertainly. Thus, in the *Tugendlehre*, he is not averse to the use of powerful and comprehensive metaphor. For instance, discussing 'practical' in contradistinction from 'pathological' love, he likens it to the operation of gravitational force, at once attractive and repulsive. We are drawn towards those we love, and seek to enclose them within our own orbit, yet we acknowledge also a duty to keep our distance from them. We must not seek to impose upon them ourselves and our vision of the world. Similarly, we must not allow ourselves to be overwhelmed by an obsessive infatuation with the one for whom we suppose ourselves to care greatly. Respect is fundamental to love. Kant's use, in this passage, of the imagery of a gravitational field, is vivid and arresting. Yet we should call his use of the image dispensable to his exposition, however certainly the latter is advanced by its employment. One must distinguish such a concession from those he makes in the course of his writing on the philosophy of religion in connection with treatment of the so-called 'problem of evil'. To these matters I shall return later.

For the time being enough has been said to bring out the presence of a real split in Kant's writing, between a rigorous dismissal of the whole enterprise of speculative metaphysics, and something very different – uncertain, groping, suggestive – indicating the ways in which diverse essays towards the ineffably transcendent can, in different ways, be made servants of insight; servants in respect of whose service one must still inflexibly ask questions involving the concepts of truth and falsity. How does one, in the end, distinguish a metaphysical doctrine which is true from one which is false? Do we do so by reference to the causes which supposedly they serve? How then do we distinguish the causes? Here Kant's underlying assumption (which part of his argument is certainly intended to justify) of the primacy of the practical reason, comes to his rescue; we are by our human nature committed to that way of life whose form Kant believes the moral philosopher must seek to lay bare. At this point we have advanced beyond ambivalence. Yet, as we have seen, there is a sense in which, for Kant, metaphysical construction is a prolonged and painful disclosing of the moral order; indeed that disclosing is itself the fundamental metaphysical discovery, and the very fragility and uncertainty of structure which must beset such disclosure reflects the status of the moral order that we are laying bare. It is within this context that images achieve the significance we can properly attribute to them. Kant's contention is supremely worth while, and remains so even if we reject the formalism of his method in moral philosophy. In him we see speculative metaphysics almost converted into a series of attempts to represent the unrepresentable. He succeeds in drawing the lines between the field of description and the field of speculation, with unexampled precision, and he goes on to argue that this delimitation of frontiers is immensely to the advantage of the moral need which tempts men to suppose that there is a realm for speculation to explore. Yet, as soon as the lines are so drawn, so drawn that they seem to set men free to be at home in two worlds at once, the question of the relation of the two realms is posed – the question that cannot even be posed, let alone answered. Yet the effort to pose the question is made all the more strenuously because it is thrust upon us by that very human nature whose moral dignity Kant believed he had vindicated by his agnosticism. So we find ourselves trying to do the impossible, to find the means of saying the unsayable; for how can we significantly be said to believe that which we can in no sense understand?

Appended Note: Kant's treatment of the cosmological proof of the existence of God
It may be argued that Kant's treatment in the Dialectic of the cosmological argument is deeply effected by his conviction that it presupposes the ontological, and that if one rejects the identification of the God which this argument establishes with the *ens realissimum*, the objection collapses. It may be further pleaded that the argument moves from contingent premises relating to that which exists contingently and to the conditions under which that which comes to be has its origin, to a conclusion that is itself contingent, namely that the world has an originating cause 'which all men call God'. That there should be such an originating cause is not any sort of necessary proposition, as indeed orthodox theologians must agree because God, who is complete in himself, need not, according to long-established theological tradition, bring into being anything outside himself. Yet Kant was surely right that in speaking of divine causality and e.g.

of the causality exemplified in the occurrence of earthquakes, and of explosions, indeed of the continued operation of factors necessary for the maintenance of human and animal life, we are not speaking univocally. If we suppose that the universe took its origin in a single identifiable cosmic event of hardly imaginable dimensions, we may (speaking quite loosely) refer to such an event as the first cause in the series of events, which combined with a vast number of other factors, have brought us to our present situation. But we are enabled to use such language because for all the enormous adjustments that have to be made in respect of scale, etc. the event is still a cause in the same sense as e.g. my carelessness in the kitchen this morning combined with the facts that the coffee pot was fragile and the floor hard, issuing in the shattering of a valued household treasure. I may indeed say that if I had not been worrying, I would have taken more care in handling the object in question and that the first cause of the disaster was my reading the bad news that the post had brought. All this is perfectly intelligible, and though this example is trivial, it serves to bring out the continuity in the use of the term 'cause' in these two very different situations.

But with God's causality the matter is altogether different. We may say that we know what it is to initiate a course of action, to set in train a whole series of disastrous consequences, part foreseen and part unforeseen. But when we speak of a cause that is not simply the first in temporal order but must be regarded as the source of the entire series, including indeed both the items that fall within it and the temporal framework within which they enter into their manifold relations one with another, then we do not know what we are speaking of. God is first cause not in the sense of first in a temporal series, but in the more mysterious sense of all-originating, all-embracing, all-sustaining source. It is indeed through the divine causality that time itself is thought by the theist to come into being.

Kant was therefore right in supposing that the causal argument for the existence of God demanded that the concept of the God to which it was supposed to conclude should be given content from other sources. It is as if he were insisting that only under these conditions could we allow that the argument would enable us to reach God and not another. It is perfectly fair comment to say that Kant could have made his point plainer by a more forthright engagement with the question of the way in which he saw theistic proof rather than by way of a simple insistence that the other two proofs which he discussed presuppose the ontological. One has always to remember the insight of those who like the late Professor C. C. J. Webb insisted that the ontological argument was the most overtly religious of all the allegedly rational theistic proofs. One of its deepest assumptions must be found in the suggestion that where the concept of God is concerned, we are enabled almost immediately to reject what is clearly inadequate.

It remains, however, an important achievement on Kant's part that he criticised the suggestion that the term 'cause' was used univocally in causal argument to the origins of a disaster, or even of an event as vastly complex as an international war, and in causal argument directed towards the reference of this world to its *ultimate* source. Even if we give full weight to the insistence that metaphysically the creation of the world must be regarded as contingent, if we regard that creative act as the ultimate cause of the world, the most we are doing is to suggest a very tenuous analogy between what is familiar and what is totally unfamiliar, and between what is relative and what is ultimate. Moreover (and this is most important) if one supposes that, by his treatment of the concepts of substantial permanence and causality in the 'Analogies of Experience', as conditions of the possibility of objectively referential and descriptive discourse, Kant has established something of first-order importance concerning the role and content of these notions, the suggestion that they may be employed uncritically in transcendent metaphysics falls down. One cannot allow oneself to treat a notion which one has vindicated as indispensable for a coherent objective experience as a means whereby one may frame the relation of that world, our experience of it and our being there thus to experience to their ultimate source. For Kant it is through the concept of causality, schematised as the necessary sequence of events according to a rule, that experience of a public, objective, irreversible temporal direction is possible; he can attach no sense to a causality that cannot be bedded down in some sort of relation to this single time-order, whose irreversibility of direction imposes itself on our consciousness in the first instance through sequences of events that we suppose endowed with what in chapter 1 of this book I called an 'although' character. It is not that Kant made the ludicrous mistake of supposing that any two events of which we say that in public time the one followed the other (e.g. in the way in which the publication of this week's edition of the *Listener* follows in time my writing a letter to Ghana in reply to a former pupil's greeting, or in the way in which the beginning of the gas strike follows the completion of the first draft of this book, or in the way the ending of my lecture this morning followed at the shortest possible interval the departure of a 101 omnibus from Chesterton Road to the station, conveying two old age pensioners to their train for King's Cross) are causally connected; nor did he make the arguably equally foolish mistake of supposing that we were not very often mistaken in our first or second identification of the causes of events (as e.g. we may suppose a person's sickness due to over-indulgence in lobster, when it is in fact the manifestation of the onset of coronary thrombosis). In fact Kant had much to say on questions of concept-formation and use, on inductive inference, even on diagnosis, and he was as aware as any sensible man of the presence in human experience of fortuitous coincidences both simultaneous and successive; (although we have learnt from depth psychology to recognise how often the seemingly coincidental may be very far from fortuitous). Yet he argued most strongly that the most fundamental and sheerly indispensable role of the notion of cause in human experience was in the making it possible for us to conceive a time-order that was irreversible, proceeding within the framework of this assumption to distinguish sequences of events that were not, from those that were, connected. Thus, for him, to speak of a divine creative causality was to speak of that which only indulgence in sheer equivo-cation would allow him to characterise as causality at all.

Further as we shall see, in his reconciliation of free will and deter-minism he finds within his own philosophy, understood as a profound variation on the theme of the primacy of practical reasons, a new use for the notion of first cause, even for one that enables him to treat the causality so exercised as timeless.

6

Parable, ethics and metaphysics 1

There would be no problem of metaphysics if truth were not claimed for metaphysical statements. To say this, as we have seen, is not to deny that the problems raised by our claim to *understand* such a statement are not very serious; they are. But it is undoubtedly tempting to suppose that when we have found for such statements a special role or roles, when we have believed ourselves to have identified their function in the business of living, we have done with them and conferred on them at least a measure of respectability. A psychoanalyst undoubtedly regards as valid within the analytic situation what his patient says in 'working out' his neurosis; indeed, he would regard such speech-events as therapeutic where the patient is concerned and, in their content, revealing of his state. But a metaphysical statement is not offered as an essay in self-revelation; it is offered as an account of what is the case.

To say this is most certainly not to deny the reality of the problem of the proper vehicle of metaphysical discourse. In chapter 2, indeed, I suggested the value here of dialogue, of dialogue, moreover, which included myth, but I also insisted that if I claimed value as metaphysics for the stretch of dialogue I quoted, I did so because I claimed for it not simple profundity, but also truth. Of course, I am here thinking more of speculative than of descriptive metaphysics; the latter is a part of analytical philosophy of peculiar importance because of the pervasive import of the concepts with which it is concerned. Among these concepts Aristotle, in his *Metaphysics*, includes truth; if we insist on the claim of the metaphysician in general to say what he believes to be true, the truth he claims for his utterance is truth in Aristotle's sense. The form of his discourse may be profoundly different from that of the nuclear physicist, and the theoretical chemist, of the palaeontologist and the archaeologist; yet still he claims that what he says, properly understood, is true. It is not the expression of a mood, not a tune he whistles to keep up his courage in the dark, concerned more with the melody than with what the words say. There are also, as we have already seen, extremely important issues raised concerning the sort of necessity that the metaphysician claims for what he says; but discussion of these issues must await a further work. It will be noted that they are raised implicitly throughout this study.

In the course of this book we have often been concerned with the opposition in the theory of knowledge between what I have called 'invention', and what I have called 'discovery', the opposition between what is sometimes called 'constructivism', and what is sometimes called 'realism'. To this general topic I now return, offering some further elucidation of the concept of discovery. In July 1958, a team from Aberdeen University, under the leadership of the late Professor A. C. O'Dell, excavating a site on St Ninian's Isle, off the mainland of Shetland, lit on what afterwards became known as the 'St Ninian's Treasure'. We have no hesitation whatsoever, where such an event is concerned, in speaking of the discovery of something there to be discovered. Yet as soon as we remember the context, we realise that the archaeologically untrained could easily have destroyed, by inadvertence, what the spade had turned up. Even with the most skilled first-aid treatment, one of the articles disintegrated as a result of its exposure to the rays of the sun for the first time since, in the eighth century, supposedly under threat of Viking invasion, it had been buried. As soon as the articles of silver, both secular and religious in function, were brought to light, they all required, as a necessary condition of survival, treatment of a sort demanding the archaeologists' expertise. Moreover, very much more than first aid was required. Without the services of specialists in preservation at the British Museum, the treasure would still not have endured long: certainly not long enough to be the subject of the complex litigation that preceded its deposit in the National Museum of Antiquities at Edinburgh!

One might be tempted, therefore, to say that this discovery, this uncovering, entered into the very constitution of the objects discovered, or uncovered, in that, apart from the actual process of uncovering or discovery, they would not have survived. It is certainly true that their survival was *causally* dependent upon the circumstances of their uncovering; that is to say, their uncovering *by experts* was a necessary, though arguably not a sufficient necessary condition of their survival. It is easy, however, to go on from this to say that what survives is what has been treated, and to believe that in affirming this proposition one is affirming an identical proposition.

But this transition, I would argue, is unwarranted. Yet much more remains to be said fully to work out this example.

Thus, archaeologists in Aberdeen had made the judgement that St Ninian's Isle was worth excavating, a judgement resting on previous knowledge and previous beliefs concerning its history. Yet most certainly they did not anticipate what they found. This, although having got down below the level of the ruin of the mediaeval church on the site, they were conscious that their excavation was approaching the remains of an earlier ecclesiastical building, and that therefore findings of some sort might be anticipated of greater, even much greater, antiquity. All this serves further to emphasise the context of the discovery, and in a measure to bring out its unlikeness, from a child's chance lighting on a couple of 50p pieces on a country path; although most certainly that event is also correctly described as a discovery!

Where the St Ninian's Treasure was concerned, we might ask what precisely was discovered. I have already mentioned that some of the objects were identified as being artefacts of secular use. Yet the characterisation of others in respect of their actual function remains, even now, incomplete. Archaeologists learned in the period do not know precisely what function they fulfilled, although this ignorance in no way detracts from their appreciation of the objects' beauty. But we would none of us feel for a moment at ease if it were suggested that that discovery was a fashioning, a bringing into existence of something that was not there, because *faute de mieux* the finders called them 'pepper-pots'! I refrain from saying that we would be on edge if it were described as an invention, in as much as etymologically the word invention is derived from the Latin *inventio* – a fact by no means irrelevant to the issues with which we are concerned in this chapter. Where the St Ninian's Treasure is concerned, we are dealing with something that was unearthed – quite literally unearthed. We say this although we also realise that as soon as we begin to ask serious and detailed questions concerning both what was discovered, and its discovery, we have to say much concerning the discoverers, their skills, their problems, their training, and their good fortune.

Let us move on to a very different example. It is well known that radio-astronomers became a few years ago very interested in a new type of radio-star called a quasar. What precisely are these stars? A great deal has been written on this topic, and already a number of informed popular discussions are available. If we say that quasars are part of the total furniture of the universe, and go on from there to ask what precisely we have discovered in coming to know of their existence, we find it very hard, in giving an account of the discovery, to separate the entities that have come into the astronomers' ken from the account they give of them. It is very hard, but it is not impossible, in as much as accounts may be given that are not only revised but rejected. The entities may be categorised wrongly. They may require a new style of categorisation; yet even the new-style category must be developed out of the astronomers' existing stock, developed, but of course subject all the time to modification and correction, by observation of the ways in which these entities behave. Again we are clearly not talking of something that is brought into being; this although, in this case, *what* is discovered is a question which can only be answered, can indeed only receive precise formulation, by those technically competent in the field the discoverers have made their own. Yet, unless one is speaking with self-conscious archaism, one would not speak of quasars as inventions.

We will, of course, be told that we have to invent in order to discover; one thinks, for instance, of the advances made possible by the development of non-Euclidean systems of geometry, on the one hand, and by electron-microscopy, on the other. We shall see later examples of the extent to which something analogous may be said of literature. Yet in this last connection we distinguish the kind of invention which makes discovery possible, from the kind of invention which simply finds its end in the entertainment, both of the inventor, and the recipients of his invention. There is a difference between learning, and being entertained, or rather between learning and being merely entertained; for sometimes we can, and should, predicate 'instructive' and 'entertaining' of the same experience.

Again, to refer to a point made by the late Professor R. G. Collingwood,[1] when we speak of the discovery of *the* cause, or more modestly of *a* cause of lung cancer, what do we mean? Suppose we say that cigarette smoking is *a* cause of lung cancer (expressing ourselves quite loosely without aid of any sort of precise quantification) what are we saying? We are saying that in cigarette smoking we have laid hold of a habit or addiction whose cure will alter, perhaps decisively in a great many cases, even in the majority of cases (unless the addiction has already lasted a long time and escalated), the conditions necessary to the incidence of the disease. We do not

---

[1] In the *Proceedings of the Aristotelian Society for 1937–38*, and again in his *Essay on Metaphysics* (O.U.P., 1940).

deny that cases of carcinoma occur in which the victims are lifelong non-smokers; we simply say that in a great many cases the correlation has been established between a habit or addiction and the incidence of this disease. There are certainly factors in our human situation which we cannot alter, whose alteration would certainly reduce the incidence of the disease; but unlike these factors, the habit of cigarette smoking is within our control; this although the breaking of any addiction does require usually the technical assistance of those professionally qualified in the treatment of the addiction in question. We speak, however, of cigarette smoking as *a* cause, because it is partly within our control; we select this factor for characterisation in causal terms because we can do something about it. Yet we are justified in speaking of what we have so selected as a cause which we have discovered, because the factor is objectively connected with the incidence of the disease. We do not regard the man or woman who sets to work to cure himself, or herself, of cigarette smoking, as a superstitious crank, seeking to placate the gods by an arbitrary ascetic discipline. We speak of him or her as prudent, even as wise, and this in precisely the same sense in which we call the man prudent or wise who refuses to believe that he will be able to break the law of gravity if he walks over the edge of a cliff, when, in fact, his movements will merely continue to illustrate it!

Thus again we are emphasising the kinship between metaphysical propositions, and those propositions of which Wittgenstein insisted that they are true, if and only if something is the case. It may be that to emphasise this kinship is in itself enough to discredit them; but only if the kinship is admitted may we be said effectively to test to destruction their claim to be taken seriously. As we shall see, in the later part of this work, there is a further sense in which we have to allow that what makes them true, if indeed they are true, is not simply something that is the case, but something that we suppose to be *in some sense* necessarily the case.[2] If we may revert for the time being to the stretch of dialogue from *Republic* II (see pp. 18–20 above), we may summarise the passage as the expression of a deep intellectual perplexity, the articulation of a profound spiritual malaise. We may indeed emphasise the singular propriety of its form to its subject-matter. But we can and must distinguish the suggestion that the young men who are speaking need, in fact, some sort of therapy, whether logico-analytical or more conventionally psychological, to enable them to come to terms with their malaise, as some

[2] This though the sort of necessity in play here is matter for another study.

sort of fantastic indulgence from the suggestion that their discourse is, in some sense, referential. If we ask whether what they say is true or false, we seem a very long way removed from the simplicities of the picture theory of the proposition. To speak of their elaborate presentation of their scepticism as a picture of reality is to enlarge the use of the term 'picture' beyond the limits of easily intelligible use. Yet it may be that they are employing the only 'system of projection' open to them to express the deep inadequacies of certain forms of ethical naturalism. Later in the work Plato makes his own attempt to lay bare what it is 'out there' that they are, in fact, referring to: this because he supposes that there is something there to which they are referring, even if, to present it to ourselves in assimilable form, we have to undertake a radical reconstruction of what we suppose human knowledge to be. If we are genuinely puzzled, as Glaucon and Adeimantus are puzzled by the question of the status of the life of a Socrates or a saint, the sense or senses in which his life may be regarded as an intimation of the way in which things are, we are puzzled concerning what, if anything, we learn from his life concerning the way things are 'out there in the world', and how such learning is possible. We are not simply concerned with the role of such discussion in human life, or to recognise the poverty, or philistine aridity of a life that is not adorned or sweetened by such speculative indulgences. In other words, we admit that in metaphysical representation we are concerned with the fruits of human inventiveness, with essays, successful or unsuccessful, to 'thrust against the frontiers of language'; there is perhaps an *ars metaphysica* displayed in a kind of disciplined boldness in extending the competence of the linguistically or conceptually familiar, which is a necessary condition for any insight we may achieve. But what we seek is to discover, not to adorn the relatively unexciting flow of our prose-description of what is the case, by intrusive poetic flight and unexpected outbursts, either of lyric or of aspiration.

This chapter is advertised as concerned with the notion of parable. The term 'parable' is one extensively used by contemporary writers in the philosophy of religion, used sometimes with a sort of coy knowingness, but with an elusiveness which contrasts unfavourably with the relative precision introduced into the definition of the concept by those professionally concerned with the study of the New Testament: for instance, Jülicher, Dodd, Jeremias. Yet it must be conceded that (if my understanding of recent discussion does not deceive me), the hard-and-fast frontier once drawn between, e.g.

parable and allegory, now no longer obtains. For instance, we realise that we treat as parable the short, sharp, almost gnomic comparison between the divine compassion for the sinner, and a shepherd's concern over the lost member of his flock; or the elaborately contrived apocalyptic image developed in Matthew 25, wherein, as a shepherd dividing his sheep from his goats, the king, who seems also identified with the Son of Man, divides the agents of spontaneous, almost forgotten service of their fellows, from those who in self-conscious virtue plead that no chance for such response ever came their way to be ignored or neglected. One could indeed speak of a parabolic content in the contrast (pointed sharply by the Myth of Gyges) between perfectly just and perfectly unjust man.

The texture of the concept of parable is open; but it is of the nature of the parabolic, not simply to disturb or break the stale cake of long-ago baked moral custom, by pointing to unnoticed possibilities of well-doing, but to hint, or more than hint, at ways in which things fundamentally are. Parables are true or false; we do not mean true or false in the sense of correspondence, which we use in connection with a passport photograph or a newspaper report of an air disaster. A parable is inevitably contrived, and we must, moreover, as those examples already cited have implied, distinguish those which are in some sense allegorical, and those which are not.[3] To liken, in the end, the alleged urgent compassion of the divine to a shepherd's obsessive preoccupation with a lost sheep, or a housewife's with a pound note she has mislaid, is to illuminate the unfamiliar by reference to recognisable routines of human behaviour. Shepherds and housewives do, as a matter of fact, very often so behave. A man is distracted from the work he has to do by the sudden realisation that he has mislaid a document which can easily be one which he does not immediately need. This distraction may be thought to have an almost neurotic quality; yet such things occur every day, and if we use them to point the pattern ultimately of the divine love for the individual, we are certainly drawing on the absolutely ordinary and familiar. Yet with the shepherd's separation of sheep from goats, it is otherwise; before we are reminded of the separation of the two flocks, the context is provided by the deliberate use of a whole apparatus of apocalyptic technicalities; we are not, as in the case of possessive preoccupation with the lost or mislaid, being enticed to extrapolate a familiar aspect of our human busyness in such a way as to allow it to throw light on what is ultimate, giving us, indirectly, information concerning the

[3] The examples are treated in much more detail in the next chapter.

way in which things are. Rather, in the parable of the sheep and the goats, we are in part illuminating the ultimate by the fantastic, more accurately by the marriage of the fantastic and the familiar.

Parables are intended to inform. Yet, by their peculiar indirection they show themselves as made to the measure of those to whom they are told. While within the Thomistic tradition the supremacy in metaphysics of the so-called analogy of proper proportionality (deriving from the influence of Cajetan's *de Analogia Nominum*) emphasises objectively recognisable correspondences between a relation between two terms familiar to us on the one hand and (for instance) the relation of creatures to creator on the other, where parables are concerned we have to deal with that which is, in its very content, subtly adapted to the individual's situation. We might even ask whether a parable is falsified if the one to whom it is spoken is almost inevitably encouraged to learn the wrong lessons from it, to 'get it wrong'.[4]

In this form of discourse there is something intensely individual, and this intense individuality effects the peculiar sort of indirection which characterises the parable's reproduction of what it affirms to be the case. To a considerable extent this is a matter of context. There is no formula for the interpretation of a parable, as conceivably it could be claimed that there are rules determining which analogate is most appropriately represented by this or that analogy of proper proportionality: so that this or that analogy becomes the stereotype or formula for construing this or that metaphysical or theological belief. Yet, in such cases the belief comes first, and the resources of the analogy are invoked to render it in a measure intelligible, whereas a parable is meant to hint or suggest that which transcends. There is an element of creative selectivity involved in its choice and development governed, no doubt, by what the teller hopes to suggest; but where the hearer is concerned, the assimilation of what he hears, in terms of his own experience, is an acknowledgement of the frontiers of his aspirations, which remains peculiarly his own – this though, if the parable is effectively parabolic, it will operate not simply as a stimulus to action, whether by its incentive force or by the inculcation of real or imagined guilt but by an addition to, or transformation of, his beliefs about the world.

The precise relation of this sort of discourse to other kinds of which we would say without hesitation that they enlarge our stock

---

[4] Anyone influenced by the late Professor J. L. Austin might rather call its telling an inappropriate performance.

of knowledge is obscure; indeed, it is one of the central problems of this work. A man, relatively ignorant of the operations of international monetary institutions, may be fascinated to learn in detail the roles of such bodies as the International Monetary Fund, and the Bank of International Settlements, in a crisis occasioned by grave losses of gold reserves on the part, e.g., of the United Kingdom and the United States of America. Yet the novelty of the knowledge he gains (if he gains anything) through parables is another sort of novelty. Parables hint, or convey intimations; yet what they thus hint or intimate has about it the suggestion of the ultimate. Even where the near-allegory of the sheep and the goats is concerned, one can disregard as insignificant (except for the fact that it is there), the apocalyptic imagery whereby it is embroidered and still find one's most seriously held professions of value queried by its savage interrogative irony. Yet the transformation is wrought indirectly, and a man can hardly say that this and that he has learnt, even in the way in which a young man learning for the first time something, let us say, of the cost to himself and others of an easy dilatoriness, may admit that he has had a lesson.

Parables are pieces of living discourse. One would not call, for instance, the late Dr F. R. Tennant's masterly repristinisation of the traditional argument to design in the chapter 'Cosmic Teleology' in vol. 2 of his *Philosophical Theology*,[5] a parable. Here a number of propositions concerning particular aspects of the universe in which human beings find themselves, into which they are born, and in which they live, are colligated with careful argument, and so presented together as suggesting certain conclusions concerning the origin of that universe. Here we have to do with a massive argument which can be assessed, in respect both of its premises and its conclusion, and of the validity of the transition from former to latter. With parables it is altogether different; they belong to the context of a common interrogation. They are the indispensable *prolegomena* to argument, rather than its constituent elements. They suggest, they disturb, they give purchase-hold on disturbance; yet they do so by a claim to truth or falsity.

A parable may, indeed, be false; false by reason of the fact that, spoken as it is by one individual to another, he may inevitably, being the man he is, find in it the suggestion that a particular way of life to which he is already prone, is in accordance with the nature of things. So his image of himself is confirmed, not disturbed or

[5] (New ed., C.U.P., 1969.)

challenged. The ambivalence of parabolic discourse rests in the fact that it lends itself to exploitation by those who seek confirmation for their prejudices, rather than to the enlightenment of those for whom the cake of established moral and intellectual custom must be broken. So in Christ's parable of Pharisee and tax-gatherer, the latter is said to have returned home more obviously acquitted of his guilt by God through his penitence, than the former through the itemisation of the detail of his developed self-discipline. Here (to transcribe into more general terms) the worth of a real self-knowledge is set above, almost in ontological terms, that of a carefully cultivated, rigorously maintained discipline of life; indeed, the latter is presented as a means whereby a man may screen his own reality from himself.[6] Yet the parable may be received as the validation of a certain sort of emotional self-indulgence, supposedly presented in it as somehow superior to the moral energy and initiative displayed and achieved through responsible self-discipline. So reasoning one could call the parable false, or if one prefers another form of language, obscured in respect of its lesson through its form.

It is indeed this ambivalence inherent in the very 'system of projection' to which they belong which makes some parables such elusive instruments of metaphysical representation. Yet, at the same time, they have the unquestioned advantage of focussing in completely concrete terms the central metaphysical concern – that of reaching through the familiar to its alleged transcendent ground, without evacuating that familiar of its own proper dignity, without treating it, for instance, as if *alles Vergängliches ist nur ein Gleichnis*. The shepherd's and the housewife's obsessions are of the stuff of human life; but on what principle do we justify selection of these moments as parabolic, and not others? Do we not do so, knowing what we are looking for? Or is there in the parabolic that which points beyond itself, involving us willy-nilly within the relatively confined context of parabolic discourse, in the sort of formal problems concerning the representation of the relation of relative to absolute, with which we have been occupied throughout this work? To some extent, to speak in these terms is to be reminded of the familiar antithesis between *fides quaerens intellectum* and *intellectus quaerens fidem*. From the latter standpoint a very great deal in human life is capable of being interpreted in parabolic terms. Indeed, the disciplines of such interpretation, the avoidance, for instance, of the sheerly

---

[6] It may be noticed that this treatment of the parable leaves on one side crucial questions relating to the nature of faith.

arbitrary or sentimentally contrived might be regarded as an indispensable propaedeutic study for the would-be metaphysician. Yet we have to reckon with the fact that it is the case that, willy-nilly, men and women are moved to discover a parabolic quality in some of the routines of their lives, or alternatively to find by some of the great parables (for instance the shepherd and the goats, or the 'Grand Inquisitor'), their own half-crystallised insights converted into clear, wide-ranging, if deeply disturbing perceptions of the way in which things are. Such perceptions can only be analysed in terms of the application of the parable which has made them possible; that parable is not for them a mere 'go-cart' of the understanding.[7] Yet these perceptions are much more than a more wide-ranging understanding of the parable, in the sense in which such understanding might be claimed by a man who could both recount and interpret it in the sense of telling, in general terms, what it is intended to convey. Rather we have to do with perception concerning human existence or, more fundamentally, of the way in which things are, which has been made possible through the deep assimilation of the parable.

In suggesting a case where the parable, as received, should be rejected as false, we seem to find that falsity focussed in the ethical beliefs which its mistaken reception encouraged. At first sight this might be thought to imply that the truth of parables resided in the profundity of the edification which they made possible. But if they edify, they do so through what they suggest of the ways in which things are, through their fulfilment of a claim to enlarge perception, indeed to provide in themselves the instrument and expression of such enlargement, so that the man who has assimilated their lesson, and through them learned to see the world anew, is more effectively seeing things as they are.

[7] Kant called examples 'go-carts of the understanding'.

7

Parable, ethics and metaphysics II

It is of the nature of a parable that it advertises the unfamiliar by the familiar. So the story of the lost coin urges the listener to catch in the housewife's obsessive, even neurotic preoccupation with the lost piece of her housekeeping money a hint of the true pastor's pre-occupation with the defaulter, indeed of the divine concern for the individual soul. The listener is bidden recognise the paradox that the ways of God with men may be suggested by frankly irrational be-haviour. Thus in a Perthshire bar a fellow customer remarked to me some years ago, as I checked the loose change in my pocket, that it was strange one should be so fretted by the loss of a shilling and yet so ready to spend four shillings and sixpence on a large whisky. We are dealing with the familiar; yet it is made to suggest the ultimate and in the manner of its suggestion to disturb our sense of the proprieties.

Again in the climactic image of the last judgement wherewith the public teaching of Jesus is concluded in the Gospel of St Matthew the scene is set by the use of flamboyant apocalyptic terminology. The phrase *sunteleia tou aiōnos* (consummation of the age)[1] is char-acteristic of the language of the apocalyptists. Then when the judge-ment is set men and women are separated into groups as sheep from goats. On the goats is pronounced the judgement of condemnation, a judgement which they reject, questioning indeed when they saw the Son of Man in need, in sickness, or in captivity, and failed at least to try to meet that need. They are told that in as much as they failed so to serve the least of his brethren they failed to serve him. Similarly the sheep are as surprised by the judge's commendation of their service as their opposites by the condemnation of their lack at once of perception and of response. There is a supreme irony in this presentation of the final judgement upon the human scene. Both innocent and guilty are ignorant alike of the positive quality of their

[1] In the last verse of the Gospel the risen Jesus tells his disciples that he is with them till the consummation of the age.

innocence and the negative infection of their guilt. The service done to the Son of Man in the least of his brethren is something of which those who served him have been in a sense unaware. Of course they knew what they were doing in the sense that if they were asked what they were about they would have been able to characterise their action. But they would have failed to characterise it as service or failure to serve the Son of Man.

Thus, to take an example: a young man's mother had recently died and his knowledge of her character, familiarity with the detail of her behaviour, recollection of her heartless triviality, etc., rendered him capable only of unquestioning agreement with those who did not hesitate after her death to emphasise to him her worthlessness, even tracing in detail the manner of her little-minded cruelty. An old woman who had known her quite well when she was nearly at her worst, had been employed by her and had experienced her selfishness at close quarters spoke to him of her with a different voice. No one who knew this old woman could question her integrity, her inno-cence of those faults of snobbery, of empty-mindedness mingled with vanity, which had made the young man's mother the morally questionable individual she undoubtedly was. Yet this old woman spoke of the dead woman with a warmth and affection that the young man found deeply healing. By his words he was not encouraged to sentimental disregard of the truth, of the damage his mother had done to himself as well as to many others; yet by these words he was enabled to accept the judgement as bearable, to find in the woman he remembered not simply the object of a love he was ashamed of or the target of a judgement that could hardly avoid an element of the vindictive, if only in protection against the supposedly distorting prompting of a pity awakened by her memory. Indeed she was one whom he must indeed judge adversely, yet remembering even as he did so that she had left those who genuinely mourned her passing.

'You did it unto me.' We tend to think of such service too quickly in terms of response to the claims upon our concern of the old who live alone, the senile, the bedridden, the alcoholics, the methylated-spirit drinkers, the heroin addicts etc. Yet the parable would warn men particularly against the sort of careful restriction of the service of the Son of Man which would enable them to know, with the kind of exactitude with which for instance the constructional engineer may calculate the allowance he must make for wind-stress in building a bridge over the tidal estuary of a great river, precisely what sorts of action specially qualify to be regarded as service of the Son of Man, what human predicaments especially entitle victims of human cruelty or natural circumstance to be accounted his brethren, whereas the irony of the parable is a warning against precisely this sort of restriction of the area of his claim and presence, this sort of demarcation of places where his demands encounter us. If a man or woman supposes that he or she can provide exhaustive and definitive criteria for distinguishing 'the least of these my little ones' from the rank and file of humanity he has evacuated the parable of its irony. He has indeed converted it from a parable into a recipe whereby he can achieve a certain moral security, even play in his own eyes the elevating role of the saviour of mankind, the one on whose service the outcasts depend. So he passes to the side of the goats, utterly surprised by the consequence of a failure of discernment that has sprung from an artificially imposed restriction of the relevance of the imagery of the parable. Aristotle at the outset of the *Nicomachean Ethics* insists that in no field of human concern will man achieve an exactitude (*akribeia*) in excess of that which the field in question allows. So Jesus in the parable warns men that through the cultivation in morality and epistemology of an irrelevant *akribeia* they beget in their souls the lie of an outward ignorance. If the example rather elaborately developed in the course of this exposition seems somewhat trivial compared with instances of desperate human need that I might have cited, its triviality has the effect of enabling us to penetrate more deeply the parable's pervasive irony, and indeed to learn something of the role of irony in the projection of the ultimate. There is a sense in which men and women do not know what they are doing, although of course there is a sense in which they do. In my example the old woman knew perfectly well that she was speaking warmly of the dead woman she had known; yet if she had been told that she served the Son of Man she would have been embarrassed. On the other hand we have all of us known those whose proudest claim it is to be his most humble servants, quick to wash the feet of their brethren, who ensure by their devotion that they pass him unrecognised in 'the least', who are sometimes ordinary and uninteresting, absorbed in little worlds that seem empty of the high drama of what we call clamant need.

Yet this parable may be thought simply the vehicle of a profound and subtle moral teaching, the hardly expressible lesson of the universal relevance of moral principles, the unadvertised omnipresence of their demand. It employs the image of a final judgement, an absolute scrutiny, whose executive agent is variously described as the Son of Man and the king. The phrase Son of Man is again an apocalyptic term, the designation of a mysterious pre-existent being somehow revealed at the end of the age, to usher in by his action the age which is to come. The origins of the conception, and its complex pedigree in elements of the visionary experience of the prophet Daniel, in ideas born of the symbiosis of Jewish and Persian religious traditions, in the myths of the 'heavenly man', in the supersession of the more flexible aspirations of prophecy by the rigid formalised schemes of successive ages, ordered in providential necessity characteristic of the apocalypses – these need not concern us. What is relevant is the contextual proximity of this extraordinary allegory with its mention of the apocalyptic Son of Man, to the story of Christ's passion which opens with the reminder that after two days comes Passover and the betrayal of the Son of Man to crucifixion. Immediately there follows the tale of an embarrassing act of devotion performed upon him by a woman in the quiet of a friend's house, an act certainly extravagant, conceivably dangerous (there are scholars who argue that the anointing was intended as the anointing of Jesus as the Messianic King, and that the betrayal for which Judas Iscariot sought and received tangible financial reward was simply the information that this woman had acted towards Jesus in a way that was at once a confession of his Messiahship and an invitation to him to fulfil the roles that office laid upon him), almost certainly expressive of an unbalanced, ill-disciplined emotion. Yet Jesus rebukes her critics; he has been served; he will soon be dead and beyond reach of human service; yet 'the poor' (a phrase comprehensive with delicate sarcasm of the various classes of necessitous persons which one after the other supply the eager servants of humanity in general with the successive objects of their well-organised beneficent concern) will be always there. They will be always there for those who make well-doing into the central organising purpose of their lives, who will surely be able to find candidates suitable to receive the service of their energetic benefaction. And he continues by saying that this action (maybe, I say, intended as a Messianic anointing) is an anticipated preparation of his body for burial.[2] So wherever the story of his ordeal is recounted this woman will have her place in it as the one who made ready his body, even before the first blows of his enemies rained down

[2] But contrast the different and extremely important treatment of the tale in Professor David Daube's *The New Testament and Rabbinic Judaism* (Athlone Press, 1956).

upon it, for its interment. Thus her devotion intended perhaps as a flamboyant challenge to an act of self-commitment is transformed into something very different, and thereby it is suggested perhaps purified of the confusion at once of motive and of concept which informed it.

We are moving forward from the parabolic, intended simply to reveal the peculiar intractability of moral principles, the impossibility of their conversion into hard-and-fast moral rules, supplying us inflexibly with actual guidance in the field of human conduct, as if that field were somehow more restricted than life itself. There is the suggestion that the Son of Man who is served in the spontaneous response to his need, present in the need of the least of his brethren. is in the final judgement judge and also advocate. Of those who fail to confess him in time the Son of Man will, he says elsewhere, be ashamed in eternity. He will disown them altogether, eschewing his role as witness and advocate on their behalf. As they have failed to know him, he will fail to know them; and for him to know them is not simply a matter of his recognising their forgotten responses, their actual commitments in contradiction from their avowed and often publicly professed beliefs, but to take upon himself the reinterpretation of their actions, even casting them into another mould.

One could continue indefinitely. The Good Samaritan is presented as an exemplar of unfettered service. One of outcast race, he is not fettered by the grave obligations of priest and Levite. One had better say not that he is not fettered, but that he is not bound by the same rules of self-discipline; so he is able to come to the aid of the highwaymen's victim. Are we to suppose it better to be thus free of the informing discipline of a great religious tradition and to be a rootless outcast? Yet he administers first aid and then conveys the victim to an inn, leaving him to the more expert care of the proprietor and his staff, paying money and promising more should more expense be incurred in caring for the guest on his return. His first impulsive act yields to a sober and prudent provision for the man he has befriended; yet the first impulsive, even dangerous, decision to administer first aid is the necessary condition of his latter more circumspect concern. There was risk involved here. Priest and Levite avoided danger; at least they preserved their fitness to offer prayer for the victim at the hour of the evening sacrifice. One may smile; but in human life the detached prayer of the contemplative is sometimes eloquent of a profounder concern than the eager intrusions of those who are quick off the mark to help others, thinking more of the extent to which their self-esteem is preserved and enlarged by their eagerness than of the victims they seek to benefit, who are to be advantaged by their own unpractised service. No one who goes to the aid of another whom he knows to be in need, even when he sees no adequate professional assistance available, fails to run the risk of great human damage both to himself and the object of his supposedly spontaneous concern, and indeed to others bound up with both of them in the bundle of life. One learns to suspect one's motives when one feels oneself prompted to be kind, or rather to be what one would oneself half-heartedly and others more whole-heartedly call kind, mistaking for a genuine kindness something as counterfeit as artificial flowers contrasted with real. True concern for the welfare of others is something hardly won, easily lost and replaced by a destructive self-indulgence, which finds in the supposed predicament of those others and in one's own role in seeking to relieve it rich material for fantasy, interposing between oneself and others also and the reality of the human situation an impenetrable barrier.

There is a sense in which it is only when one has learnt the reality of mutual dependence, when one has outgrown the illusion of supposing that spontaneous response to human need is somehow exempt from tragic flaw, that one comes to see that such parables as that of the Good Samaritan are parabolic in pointing beyond themselves.[3] If we pursue our understanding of them to the end they advertise a human need ultimately, even as their simplicity sets an immediate question-mark against our hope to avoid the risks of human existence by carefully calculated and meticulous observance of a routine self-discipline. Of course prudence has its place in life. One's assistance is revealed as genuine by the extent to which it takes stock of the possibilities of professionally effective care. We cannot escape the complexity of the human situation, the different aptitudes, skills and virtues that the successive phases of that situation call into play. Yet prudence is not the whole of human excellence, any more than that excellence can be assured by a careful ascetic discipline imposing order on the promptings of charity. In their complexity, especially maybe in experiences that thrust us most fully into life, there is danger, and we risk damage not only to ourselves but to others. So in the midst of life in the very exercise of compassion, even the first real flickers of a true charity, we are in desperate human danger, and we crave a foundation for our conduct, not this time a vision which will authenticate through its complete reconstruction of the fabric

[3] To these issues I return later.

of human knowledge that the life of the saint is the most revealing intimation of the ultimate, but rather this time a fulfilment to which indeed in various ways the parables point. To this fulfilment they point by disturbing us as we seek to make their lessons our own. In different ways their simplicity proves deceptive; thus we are encouraged to find the hint of a transcendent presence in the obsessive time-wasting fretting of the housewife for a mislaid half-crown. If she forgets about it, her eyes or the eyes of other members of her family will surely light on it later. In our own life we know the need of self-discipline, of refusing to be distracted by the inevitable casual mislayings of this or that which mark a busy day, or a day when we allow our thoughts to wander from what we are about. Yet the obsessive preoccupation speaks of the eagerness to receive human kind that was expressed in Jesus' quickness to eat with the socially outcast, whether as their fellow or as their houseguest, and this in turn suggests the presence of a transcendent action, of which the common meal is not a mere *simulacrum*, but an effective concrete expression. So the irony in the contents of the allegory of the sheep and the goats sets a question-mark against the ease with which we confine the scope of the moral order within boundaries much narrower than will contain the extraordinary detailed complexity of human life and then goes on to hint at the peculiar role in the ultimate judgement of the human story of the Son of Man. This role indeed in its peculiarity reflects the internal contradictions between the uses of this pervasive designation. Finally the simplicity of the tale of the Good Samaritan, told to enable a man to recognise neighbourliness for what it is by discerning its practice, is shown not as deceptive but as a simplicity achieved against the background of the necessary and the threatening complexities of human existence. The immediacy of response is made relatively secure by subsequent prudence: yet in itself it is precarious and the sort of stretch of human life typified by the Samaritan's action is pregnant with the hint of possible tragedy. It is indeed a commonplace of Christian perception to emphasise that very often it is only the man or woman who is made overwhelmingly aware of the depth of our involvement one with another in mutual dependence for good and ill who learns to say *ex animo* the lines of the traditional evangelical hymn 'nothing in my hand I bring, simply to thy cross I cling'.

Parables certainly move on the frontiers of the transcendent although the transcendent in question is at first sight vastly different from the Platonic 'idea of the Good', in whose vision his revisionary reconstruction of human knowledge is complete. They so move by what they say, by what they are understood as saying, by those who quickly respond to the system of projection 'on which they are set'. There may be thought to be a particular language game in play in the narration and in the response to the parabolic. One could conceive oneself plotting the highly flexible rules of parabolic communication whereby their peculiar sense within the parabolic game is given less by the individual expressions than by the successive stages of the parable, the distinguishable layers of its exposition. So in the allegory of sheep and goats one distinguishes the clear assertion that men and women are ultimately judged good or evil by the depth, the range, the spontaneity (above all the spontaneity) of their response to the needs of others, the irony which insists that this service to be genuine must be unrecognised for what it is, invested with such a quality of ordinariness that it passes almost unremembered, certainly never invested by the agent with the high dignity with which the professional ecclesiastic often invests his professional work on behalf of the institution which provides his salary, or even with the kind of mock-humble suggestion of self laid on the altar of service, which one has heard highly-placed lay servants of their church (often more 'ecclesiastical' than archbishop, bishop, dean or vicar) use to characterise their lives: 'I serve the church.' The sharp irony involved in the claim that moral and religious perception is always in a measure unconscious is then further qualified by the contextually adjacent narrative of the woman who served Jesus on the threshold of his ordeal by coming beforehand to make ready his still unburied body for burial. Such quick movement from level to level is involved in the hearer and reader of parables who play the language games of hearing and reading parables, who would not confuse the parabolic with the language of rapportage, with poetry, even with tragic drama or with fiction (yet here as we shall see the frontier of demarcation is hardly drawn) who might indeed go on to find the special role of the parabolic in its disturbing qualities, in its inducement of a kind of self-knowledge. For instance, when the moralist Joseph Butler, who rejected Wollaston's identification of all virtue with truthfulness, and truthfulness itself with rational consistency in action, came in his sermons in the Rolls Chapel to deal with self-deceit, he referred to Nathan's confrontation with David, following the latter's infatuation with Bathsheba, and his plot to make her his wife by giving her husband Uriah the chance to distinguish himself in service of king and country by being thrust into a place of mortal danger in the hour of battle. The masquerade is played out to the end, yet Butler with his awareness of the deep complexity of human nature, finds the first beginnings of the masquerade in sexual passion issuing in destructive infatuation. For David will conceal the adulterous quality of his passion by making it possible through murder for him to marry Bathsheba and the quality of murder as murder he will conceal by disguising it as the offering to a devoted soldier of opportunity for supremely significant because supremely dangerous service of his king. It is by means of his parable of the ewe lamb that Nathan first elicits from David his personal and royal condemnation of a comparable invented act of covetousness. Then when the king has said that such men as the thief of the poor man's ewe lamb deserve the supreme penalty Nathan directly identifies the king as the one whose guilt he has indirectly constrained him to acknowledge. Thus the king now grasps the principle he has violated. Here the disturbing effect of parabolic discernment is clear. It shatters the veil of self-induced pretence whereby David has hidden from himself what he is about.

No utilitarian could fail to admit the validity of such discourse regarded as a tool for the effective shattering of the necessarily destructive webs woven in self-deception by men who have failed to come to terms with themselves. If the utilitarian rejects as sterile an obsessive preoccupation with motive and intention, if he accepts the sovereign authority of the greatest happiness principle as the yardstick for measuring public and private policies of life, by the same yardstick he is not only permitted but even constrained to welcome styles of discourse that inhibit the continuance by human agents of courses likely to be destructive both to themselves and to their fellows. Similarly the utilitarian might welcome parables that check human readiness to conceive in too narrow terms the possibilities of service of their fellows (construed in terms of the increase in the total quantum of human happiness) which inherited traditions of moral discipline, even too narrowly conceived policies of human welfare, might induce them to overlook.

The cake of custom requires ultimately to be broken. This is surely an important, even a primary, maxim of utilitarian ethics. The premises on which its authority rests comprise statements both singular, particular and general concerning the extent to which in human history, for instance, the various élites required by the productive and technical realities of successive societies have sought to give sacrosanctity to their role, to render inviolable their historic prestige and to perpetuate as absolute norms the adjustments valid only in the name of that human happiness which for a while they safeguarded and through whose advance for a while the élites in question earned for a period their peculiar dignity. The settlement which yesterday emancipated human enterprise from the bondage of an entrenched tyranny and provided the disciplines required to direct it aright towards the maximisation of human happiness today itself restricts our opportunities of well-doing, and distorts our perception of the actualities of the human situation. And here of course the dissatisfied Socrates finds his indispensable role. So too the quizzical insinuating interrogation of the parabolic.

But for the utilitarian it is a parabolic discourse that is justified by its human function. It is a form of discourse that we find an indispensable tool for discernible human purposes. It is not a parabolic which when taken in relation to the supposed ultimate context of reference raises the question of the truth and falsity of what is said; the disturbance it effects is a relative disturbance and there are canons for measuring its utility. Clearly a sovereign who exploits his prerogatives to contrive murder endangers more than his reputation. He threatens the institution of government, encouraging also among the lawless a desperate cynicism which may outweigh as a determinant of their behaviour the cautious self-restraint imposed by a recollection of the likelihood of detection and punishment. His action is a standing invitation to the desperate who are clearly half in love with the conceit of a challenge to the built-in stabilities of their social milieu. Such a sovereign must as an individual be brought to self-awareness.

But there are other sorts of disturbance which might be judged sterile, the kinds of disturbance occasioned in a man who is moved to ask questions concerning the way in which the quick relation of the parabolic to its total contextual frame and the taking of both together may provide a movement of approach to the transcendent, to the transcendent that is affirmed to be present to men. And here we are immediately reminded of the crucial issues raised by the frankly agnostic conclusion of chapter 5.

8

Return to Plato and Aristotle

In the last two chapters I was concerned with the notion of parable, and it is against this background that I wish now to return to the notion of the transcendent. For it is this notion which, more than any other, enables us to fasten on the central issue of this work. No one would deny the extent to which parabolic discourse may illuminate human life by inducing deeper self-criticism, by puncturing make-believe, by renewing simplicity, etc. Yet, the crucial question remains whether, by means of parable, myth, saga, etc., we are enabled to make significant statements concerning that which lies beyond the frontiers of conceivable experience.

Earlier in this work attention was directed towards the notion of degrees of being, in the form which it was encountered in Aristotle's *Categories* and *Metaphysics*, a form which, it was implied, if not explicitly agreed, was largely empty of all direct speculative importance. Where parables were concerned it was implied, if not directly stated, that the context out of which they sprang and to which they belonged was very often a deep, even if unacknowledged, ethical perplexity which indeed it was part of a parable's function to articulate, even to work out. In this chapter an effort will be made to bring together these two discussions. In Aristotle's table of categories, the category of substance in the sense of 'first substance', whether understood as concrete entity or as form, transcends all other categories in that in all predication some reference to substance is presupposed. When we say of Socrates that he is a man, we are predicating of him in the category of substance; if we say that he is a philosopher, we are predicating in the category of quality; if we say that he is snub-nosed, we are predicating in the category of accident. There is a perfectly intelligible sense in which his being a man transcends his being snub-nosed in the sense that he cannot be snub-nosed without being a man, while he may be a man without being snub-nosed. So we say that the status of his manhood is ontologically superior to that of his snub-nosedness etc. All this is little more than

94

repetition. We have here a very special sense of dependence, clearly assumed by Aristotle in his doctrine of category, and indeed by such a twentieth-century philosophical master as the late Professor G. E. Moore in his criticism of the thesis maintained in some form by many, if not all, idealist logicians that all relations are internal to their terms.[1] In his criticism of this doctrine Professor Moore availed himself of Aristotle's distinction between predication in the category of substance and predication in the category of accident, showing by his use of this distinction, in a quite novel connection, its permanent significance and power. The sort of dependence in play here is unique. It requires to be distinguished very carefully from the sort of dependence that we claim to obtain between an event, say a sudden explosion, and the event or complex of events that we pronounce its causal ancestor or ancestors. Again it is a dependence of a quite different order from that of the truth of a true function on the truth of one or more of the propositions of its range. If I say that someone in this room is feeling the heat, the truth of that proposition depends on that of one or more of a number of propositions whose subjects are supplied by terms referring directly to the persons at present in this room. Only if one such proposition is true is the proposition – someone in this room is feeling the heat – true. Again, if I say that everyone in this room is feeling the heat that proposition is true if and only if a whole set of singular propositions whose subjects are supplied by terms referring to persons at present in this room, are all of them true. If we are guilty of excessive sophistication in treating general statements as truth functions and ignoring their roles in ordinary conversation, such sophistication may be justified in this context where we are concerned to bring out the differences between the sorts of dependence with which we are familiar in human discourse. Aristotle's doctrine of categories, and other doctrines of categories which in some measure show its inspiration, compels us to recognise a sort of hierarchical dependence in our concepts. What exactly Aristotle meant by the being-*quâ*-being, which he regarded as the subject-matter of metaphysics, remains ultimately obscure. But if we may temporarily avert from exploring the depths of that obscurity, we may suggest a caricature that illuminates as well as distorts its subject-matter by saying that Aristotle distilled from Plato's complex and many-sided theory of forms certain highly significant insights into the nature of conceptual order. One could

[1] 'Internal and External Relations', in G. E. Moore (ed.), *Philosophical Studies* (Routledge and Kegan Paul, 1922).

even say that he substituted the prose of analysis for the poetry of speculation. There remains great insight in the dictum Coleridge borrowed from Goethe that everyone of us is at bottom either a Platonist or an Aristotelian. The very phrase 'degrees of being', suggests at first to the hearer, if not the metaphysical foundation of a hierarchically-ordered society, at least that kind of movement from the many to the one, that sort of dedicated pursuit of an ultimate all-embracing comprehension, that ascent from the familiar to the unseen which characterises the mood of the dialogues of Plato's middle period. It may seem surprising, almost paradoxical, to say that we find in Aristotle a doctrine of degrees of being which has been rendered almost totally aseptic through conversion into a systematic exploration of the working of our most fundamental concepts, such notions as thing and property, existence, truth, etc. Yet, such a view is highly defensible. If the contrast between Aristotle and Plato is often found to lie in the former's deep concern with empirical observation, it also resides in the latter's minute and concentrated attention to complex, intractable detail that puts a question-mark against his own most cherished constructions. Thus, classification by reference to genus and species was of the greatest importance to Aristotle, and it is his readiness to recognise the deep limitations of such a scheme where our most fundamental concepts are concerned, and indeed where empirical study of the world around us is at issue, that marks his genius.

We may find a significant example of the contrast between Aristotle's philosophical style and Plato's if we attend to a very well-known passage of Plato's *Republic* which has particular relevance to our purpose in that it is concerned with the transcendent. I refer to the analogy of the sun in *Republic* VII, in which Plato seeks to apply the relation of the form of the Good to the other forms, and of the way in which through vision of the former, knowledge of the latter is perfected.

> This, then, which gives to the objects of knowledge their truth and to him who knows them his power of knowing, is the Form or essential nature of Goodness. It is the cause of knowledge and truth; and so, while you may think of it as an object of knowledge, you will do well to regard it as something beyond truth and knowledge and, precious as these both are, of still higher worth. And, just as in our analogy light and vision were to be thought of as like the Sun, but not identical with it, so

here both knowledge and truth are to be regarded as like the Good, but to identify either with the Good is wrong. The Good must hold a yet higher place of honour.

You are giving it a position of extraordinary splendour, if it is the source of knowledge and truth and itself surpasses them in worth. You surely cannot mean that it is pleasure.

Heaven forbid, I exclaimed. But I want to follow up our analogy still further. You will agree that the Sun not only makes the things we see visible, but also brings them into existence and gives them growth and nourishment; yet he is not the same thing as existence. And so with the objects of knowledge: these derive from the Good not only their power of being known, but their very being and reality; and Goodness is not the same thing as being, but even beyond being, surpassing it in dignity and power. (Cornford's translation)

Plato is most certainly concerned in this passage with the transcendence not simply of the world of particulars by the world of forms, but of the world of forms itself by the Good. He is concerned to lay bare that ultimate which in the *Republic* he is in some sense seeking, and he does this in a way that remains interesting and illuminating for all its familiarity. Earlier in this work space was devoted to discussion of the second book of the *Republic* and with the passage in the second book then discussed at greatest length, in my judgement the analogy of the sun is closely linked. Of this more later. For the present it is the style that we must fasten on.

In the analogy of the sun, Plato is concerned to deploy the ultimate, to deploy that indeed which transcends the transcendent, and the language he uses oscillates between the sheerly lyrical and the formally precise throughout this passage. Thus the style which immediately follows his invocation of the sun as the source of light is pervasive. Yet at the same time we can trace clearly in this passage the sharply defined form of what later Aristotelian schoolmen (for instance Cajetan) called an analogy of proper proportionality. As the world of coming to be, of growth and of nurture, is to the sun, so the world of the intelligible, the world whose mode of being is characterised by Plato as existence and essence, is to the Good. As the sun makes possible coming to be and growth and nurture, modes of being that are temporal but are inconceivable except as coming to be and passing away, so to the timeless world of the intelligible, its being and essence, is provided by the Good. Plato insists that the

Good is not itself being but transcends being, both in dignity and in power. Yet it is important to notice how precisely Plato's analogy can be set out in formal terms as one of proper proportionality. As the sun to the world of becoming, so is the idea of the Good to the world of the intelligible. Through our familiarity with the former relation, we may begin to grasp the ultimate dependence in which the forms stand to the Good; this, while all the time remembering that the world of becoming itself depends asymmetrically on the world of the intelligible. Plato's purpose in using this analogy is to enable his readers to represent for themselves that ultimate on which the forms depend, approaching it indirectly but by a sort of double indirection, compelling his readers to recognise that they can at least make something of the sort of dependence in which forms stand to the Good, by analogy with the familiar fact of the dependence of the life of the world to which they belong upon the sun. Yet, if his primary aim is expository, what makes the exposition legitimate is the ontological dependence of the world of particulars upon the forms and the world of forms upon the Good. The system of the world of particulars is grounded in that of the world of forms, and the system of the world of particulars depends upon the sun, and this latter dependence finds its ground in the world of forms which correspondingly depends upon the Good. In my view, this passage, read in close conjunction with the long passage from Book II, already discussed, belongs to Plato's attempt in the *Republic* to deploy the form of a new *paideia* through which men would be enabled to see that understanding and goodness do not fly apart and that in fact Socrates has by his way of life found the key to the gates of understanding. Although Plato's hostility to poetry is notorious and the grounds of that hostility set out earlier in the dialogue, at this stage in his exposition he invokes the resources of imagery to represent what cannot be directly conveyed, fusing what is almost embarrassing by its unrestrained lyricism with what is also formally precise.

Moreover, there is less inconsistency here than might appear. Plato's hostility to Homer and to the tragedians had many roots, ethical and metaphysical; but for our purposes here we should recall that Plato was the avowed enemy of poetry, particularly because he found in poetic *mimēsis* something that must distract men from moving to the one that stands over against the many, the all-embracing, all-subduing transcendent unity, encouraging them rather to deepen their awareness of the familiar by extending the range of examples set before them of what was possible as well as actually in the world around them. If we may temporarily disregard the controversies inevitably aroused by Plato's political theory in the *Republic*, he shows himself in that work a man obsessed by the conviction that there is a single central human problem that demands an answer at once practical and theoretical, namely the problem of the way in which a man must lead his life, a problem that only finds solution through a vision that is at once single and all-embracing, for whose achievement a man must be prepared to sacrifice all else. Plato is not an idealist. But it is a significant commonplace that he claims to stand in the tradition of a master for whom the proper study of mankind was man and for whom therefore human gropings as gropings after the ultimate, were intrinsically significant. It is the fundamental paradox of Plato's ethics in the *Republic* that by his attempt there to establish the status of such gropings and to find means whereby they may be converted into a kind of science of the ultimate, he threatened the dignity that seems to belong to individual, conscientious struggling. And yet the climax of the allegory of the cave is the philosopher's constraint to return.

It is of course notorious that in his later dialogues Plato turned his back on the grandiose metaphysical project of the *Republic* and devoted his energies to less exalted but arguably more profitable explorations. It was part of his genius that, for instance, in the *Parmenides* he showed himself sharply alive to the sheer ambiguity of the notions of presence, resemblance and participation which he had used to represent the relation of the world around us to the world of forms. Yet, beneath his powerful and rigorous criticism, devastatingly agnostic in its conclusions concerning the worth of these concepts in this connection, the hold upon his imagination of a central vision is strong; this vision is one of the many pointing towards the one in which those many find their ground, and it underpins and directs all his thinking. We must be on guard, he implies, against the pervasive temptation of anthropomorphism. We must see that that way lies inadmissible contradiction; we must learn and relearn the purgative effect of such recognition, making our own the lesson that in speculation the last enemy is anthropomorphism rather than agnosticism, yet sustained always by a sense that the underlying insights of which the theory of forms is an exploration are significant and important, and that the proper mode for the expression of this theory is always or nearly always dialogue rather than treatise.

In the sixth chapter of the first book of his *Nicomachaen Ethics*,

Aristotle submitted Plato's doctrine of the idea of the Good to a dense and many-sided criticism. It is no accident that in the case of this criticism he invokes his doctrine of categories, insisting that goodness is predicated in all the categories. If we say that God is good, we are predicating in the category of substance. But we also predicate goodness in other categories when, for instance, we say that next year will be a good time in which to allocate funds to a particular research project or that a particular area is a good one, both strategically and tactically, in which to entice an enemy to give battle in time of war. Again, we may say of a man that his many human deficiencies leave unaffected his excellence as a mathematician. Aristotle goes on to ask how then are goods to be regarded as forming a unity and he makes some extremely interesting suggestions towards an answer to that question, even though he hardly seems to develop them to the extent one would have wished. All the time in this passage he is also waging war against Plato's claim that there is some single, all-embracing vision giving a man the power to act well both in public and private in all the changing and various circumstances of human life, but indispensable in as much as only through attaining it is such human expertise at all possible. Aristotle writes as one who knows well that human life is not like this, that there are many fields in which the visionary inevitably fails and the practical man succeeds; moreover, a reference to his *Politics* shows that he is every bit as much aware of the humanly destructive consequences that threaten any attempt directly to impose upon the raw material of ordinary human lives one's own vision of the way in which those lives should be ordered. In government Plato's obsession with unity, with the achievement of a kind of *homonoia* which would banish forever the threat of civil strife, could in the circumstances of actual human life issue in a tyranny as humanly perilous as that achieved by any demagogue. It is characteristic of Aristotle that his criticisms of this central Platonic dictum are at one and the same time ontological, logical and ethical. If we emphasise the last, it is because Aristotle's argument here illuminates much that is most characteristic in his treatment of the transcendent.

The late Professor A. E. Taylor remarked that where the relation of Aristotle to Plato is concerned, we have to deal with the rewriting by a biologist of the philosophy of a mathematician. It would be a very serious mistake to forget that, where his cosmology is concerned, Aristotle achieves his own variant on the Platonic dualism. Both in his work in the *Physics* and his work on *Coming-To-Be and Passing-*

Away and in the fascinating section of the *Metaphysics* devoted to the subject of God, Aristotle shows himself very much concerned with the *suprasensible* and its relation to the world around us. But the same philosopher continually shows commitment to a strenuous attempt to conjure out of Plato's poetry the bare fruit of profound conceptual insight, and of this aspect of his work we find in the doctrine of the categories (for all its confusion) a profoundly significant example. It is from this doctrine that Aristotle's insights into some of the many interesting sorts of conceptual grouping have sprung, the sorts of insight that modern philosophers tend to discuss under the rubric of 'focal meaning'.[2] He suggests that goods may be one through derivation from a common source or through contribution to a single end, throwing the hint out without elaboration. But the reader of his *Metaphysics* has already in his discussion of the 'Idea of the Good' been reminded of the relativity of all forms of being other than substance to substance. It is almost as if Aristotle has thrown out this suggestion for students of his *Ethics* to make what they will of it and for those who follow to take it up and convert to their own use.

May I here invoke a modern illustration which I owe to the late Dr Friedrich Waismann? Suppose we ask what Euclidean geometry, that structure of supposedly necessary truths established non-inductively concerning the structure of the space presupposed in Newtonian mechanics, has in common with a modern geometry which, according to Waismann and indeed to others, we radically misunderstand if, averting from its character as a hypothetico-deductive scheme, we bewilder ourselves by seeking to incorporate into its deployment an element of intuitive interpretation of its axioms. We must, Waismann said, answer that question historically by indicating the pedigree of modern non-Euclidean geometries, while we sharply differentiate them when regarded as parts of mathematics from the way in which we must regard them when looked at as parts of physics, enabling us, for instance, comprehensively to classify measurements, etc. As parts of mathematics they are geometries almost by grace of a kind of traceable succession to Euclid, even though the proliferation of non-Euclidean systems, the outcome of the crisis of geometrical intuition and the sharp severance of pure from applied geometry (all unknown to Euclid) has changed the sense of them out of all recognition.

Here it may be claimed that any sense of degree of being, even

[2] The phrase is that of Professor G. E. L. Owen.

in the speculatively vacuous sense of Aristotle, has gone. Indeed, what is suggested is continuous rather with Aristotle's illustrations in the *Metaphysics* than with his doctrine. It may even be regarded as the next stage in the dilution of the notion of the transcendent, a stage that Aristotle was prevented by his conservatism and, indeed, by the circumstances of the age in which he wrote, from reaching. Geometries, according to Waismann, are grouped together by a kind of loose historical dependence upon Euclid, a kind of dependence which an historian of mathematics, I presume, would succeed in bringing out. Certainly, Aristotle was alive, and increasingly alive, to the significance for thought of this kind of classification. For him of course its supreme exemplar was the classification of forms of being around and upon the category of substance. A modern student may avoid, if he so desires, the descriptive metaphysical foundation of Aristotle's insight, and avail himself rather of that grasp of conceptual order which Aristotle succeeded in developing. We have already insisted that it is a commonplace to say that Plato was obsessed by the need to move from the many to the one and that Aristotle thought to counteract this preoccupation or obsession with a proper pluralism. Yet, Plato in the end would avoid monism, though the existence of the world of particulars is ontologically dependent upon that of forms. For ethically, that world of particulars was the place in which men's lives were cast, and indeed it is to that world that his philosophers, when their education is complete, must return. Yet, if Plato is not a monist, Aristotle is not a pluralist. He too is concerned with the relations of the many to the one, concerned in ways that make it possible for him to teach us a great deal concerning the manner in which our discourse actually works. His contribution to the question of the point of departure of transcendent metaphysics is ambiguous. He has a transcendent metaphysics, a theology, and one can claim that for him its starting-point is provided by the phenomenon of motion as he understood it. Yet, at the same time he sought to render aseptic the notion of transcendence to enable us to receive that notion as the crystallisation of a set of insights concerning the interrelation of various sorts of discourse. Certainly the notion of dependence in Plato's and indeed in Aristotle's cosmology is used in very different ways to bring out the dependence of this world, in Plato's case in respect of its being, in Aristotle's in respect of its motion upon suprasensible existents variously conceived. But in Aristotle, as we have seen, there is this other sort of transcendence, which belongs to, and is found in, the world of conceptual order. It is in respect of hierarchy in the world of human discourse that Aristotle makes some of his most important discoveries, or at least suggestions of the ways in which such discoveries may be made. Is there one sort of discourse that transcends all others in that this sort of discourse is woven into the texture of every other sort of utterance? Aristotle, in his doctrine of categories, seems to give in formal terms an affirmative answer to this question. But we have to ask ourselves whether the matter may not admit of other styles of treatment.

9

Empiricism and transcendence

Kant believed the metaphysician to be concerned to answer three questions: What am I? Where did I come from? What may I hope for? Such a temper is repudiated by positivistic empiricists who, and here I speak the language of fact, find it intolerable. Yet in the remarkable Gifford Lectures which he delivered before Aberdeen University,[1] Professor Michael Polanyi suggested that the kind of preoccupation of which I am now speaking could, if properly disciplined, be fertile in promoting rather than hindering fundamental investigations. The discipline was essential and it could be argued that the preoccupation had become before the end something recognisably altogether different from what we are presently considering. But Polanyi's reconciliation of science and religion (for that is in fact what he attempts in his work) takes the shape of showing that effective 'know-how' cannot long survive the atrophy of a developing tradition whose successive phases are linked by a continuing sense of the mystery of the human pursuit. To these issues we paid some attention in chapter 4 of this work and we must now return to them.

For the present I would repeat that those who put such questions as the positivists have put often share, more than they realise, a fundamental attitude with some of the metaphysicians against whom they are protesting. They fail to see that there is a sense in which they share with some of those whom they criticise a kind of indifference to the minutiae, for instance, of human experience, to the manifold diversity of human life, even to the complexities of the moral life itself. Thus it is often said of the utilitarian whether of Shaftesbury whom Butler criticised in his *Dissertation on the Nature of Virtue* or of Bentham himself, that he makes prudence (in Bentham's case, nearly identified with rational benevolence) sovereign among the virtues. One might therefore say that a man who refuses this supremacy to prudence is by that alone rejecting utilitarianism.

[1] *Personal Knowledge* (Routledge and Kegan Paul, 1958).

Now, in this century we have learned, if nothing else, to suspect the cult of the heroic, the exaltation of the life of ascetically disciplined endurance in an alleged common service over that which would allow itself to be judged by reference to more mundane concern for simply identifiable human happiness. The way of near-absolute obedience is the way that helps make possible the Belsens, the Dachaus and the Auschwitz's of the twentieth century. There is indeed an element of paradox that the contribution to ethics by some at least of those Christian thinkers most concerned to be *avant-garde* should peter out in vacuous arguments on behalf of what is called radical obedience. No virtue is surely more deeply questionable than obedience. We have to allow that much (though not all) which attracts the metaphysically-minded in the field of ethics, by reason of its rejection of utilitarianism, emerges on close scrutiny as an attitude deeply tainted by an uncritical cult of the heroic individual, or indeed something worse. (One finds such an attitude clearly exemplified in the nineteenth century in the ethical writings of Thomas Carlyle.)[2] The rejection of the ethics of Jeremy Bentham may indeed, must indeed, spring from a sense that there is more in heaven and earth than his philosophy may dream of, more in the labyrinthine wanderings of the human mind than James Mill would ever bring to light. Yet there is great danger in the path of the man who, concerned with the mysterious frontier questions of human existence, seeks to safeguard their eligibility for deep consideration by facile dismissal of utilitarianism as the morality of the cash register, or as the doctrine which erects prudence into a sovereign place among the virtues. To write in these terms is in no sense to belittle the kinds of critique achieved classically by Butler on the one hand and by Charles Dickens in his novel *Hard Times* on the other. Rather it is to make oneself aware (as Butler indeed was aware before Bentham had put pen to paper) of the dialectical character of ethical reflection.

The great painter, Paul Cézanne, took his profession very seriously, as seriously as any businessman, doctor or lawyer, devoting himself exclusively to it, working with tremendous energy. His integrity was absolute, and he made no concessions to public taste or fashion at any time in his work. Deeply cultivated and widely read, he related all his artistic experience in the fields either of music or of

---

[2] One is not surprised to find the Carlyleans, unlike John Stuart Mill, quick to spring to the defence of Governor Eyre. It is in such schools that in an English 'Dreyfus Affair' English anti-Dreyfusards would have learnt their arguments.

literature to painting. Far from wishing to depreciate tradition, he responded to, and ceaselessly studied, the work of the old masters, copying and sketching in the Louvre daily when he was in Paris. Yet in a letter dated 12 May 1904, he wrote to his friend, Emile Bernard, 'The Louvre is a good book to learn from, but it must only be an intermediary. The real and immense study that must be taken up is the manifold picture of nature.' This sentiment he developed in a further letter to Bernard written the next year, in which he said, 'The Louvre is the book in which we learn to read. We must not however be satisfied with retaining the beautiful formulas of our illustrious predecessors. Let us go forth to study beautiful nature, let us try to free our minds from them, let us try to express ourselves according to our personal temperaments. Time and reflection, moreover, modify little by little our vision and at last comprehension comes to us.'[3]

These brief remarks on Cézanne's attitude to his work in a measure confirmed by the quotations from his letters, may at first seem an intrusion into the development of my argument. But the attitude which the summary conveys expresses what can only be called a preoccupation with the transcendent. In the second letter to Bernard which I have quoted, the artist speaks of time and reflection modifying, little by little, our vision and 'thus comprehension comes to us'. The next year, in a letter to his son dated 8 September, he takes up the same theme, 'Finally I must tell you that as a painter I am becoming more clear-sighted in front of nature, but that with me the realisation is always very difficult. I cannot attain the intensity that is unfolded before my senses. I have not the magnificent richness of colouring that animates nature. Here on the edge of the river, the movements are very pretty; for the same subject seen from a different angle gives a subject for study of the highest interest and so varied that I think I could be occupied for months without changing my place, simply bending a little more to the right or the left.'

As one would expect, Cézanne's letters abound in profound reflection on the artist's life and work as he had experienced it in himself. It may indeed seem philistine to bring the brooding fulfilled so triumphantly under the rubric of preoccupation with the transcendent. But if one profoundly ignorant of the business of painting may be permitted a comment, it is impossible to read these letters and in their light to look again at the paintings to which they refer, and indeed to study the composition of the paintings in question,

[3] Cézanne's letters.

without finding here an attitude vigorously complex in its fusion of traditional schooling and creative insight, fulfilled in a sort of organisational mastery both of subject and of materials, and at the same time intense concentration of attention on the actuality to be realised on the canvas. It is the fusion of high intelligence and technical mastery with reverent scrutiny that is almost classically conveyed in the letters from which I have selected these very few quotations.

The preoccupation is of course manifested in Cézanne's way of life as well as in his experience of the world around him. The latter is at once the condition of his painting, especially it would seem, after 1870, and something developed in and by means of that painting itself. It does not seem quite right, in fact it seems very wrong, to say that Cézanne perceived thus and thus and so he painted. Yet it does seem to me right to say that it is in the end impossible that he could have perceived in the way in which he perceived and not have been the painter that in fact he was. Indeed, it was because he was a painter and the painter that he was that his perceptual experience achieved the complexity and the subtlety which undoubtedly marked it out from the awareness of less disciplined and less creative spirits. His commitment to his art (the schooling in the book of the Louvre) was a necessary condition of that experience. Yet, without that experience, and most references to it show that he could write of it in ways most interesting to the philosopher of perception, he would not have been able to paint as he did. One could indeed, where he is concerned, speak without abuse of words of a preoccupation with that which transcends because it goes beyond easy perception. And by easy perception I mean both the awareness of the natural seen by ordinary men and women and also the kind of enhanced awareness that a knowledge of Cézanne's work may make possible for them. His experience indeed elicited from him an account of the way in which he perceived what he was painting, that is a subtle variation on the familiar Kantian theme of the interplay of sense, imagination and understanding; in him we find an awareness of imagination and understanding closely relating one with another, yet distinguishable one from another, spontaneous, selective and in a measure constructive. Through this complex activity (and it is no criticism of the artist to say that the philosopher can present more formally what he proved on his pulses) Cézanne sought to come to terms with a nature he understood almost intuitively as something over against himself, something existing in its own right, and not simply as a medium into which he could project and through projection realise or exteriorise his own feelings and fantasies. Indeed (and this is surely crucial) it is the very externality of the natural world, its sheer objectivity that his intense disciplined effort alone makes it possible for him to realise. What is paradoxical is that he invokes resources of imagination, of spontaneously initiated constructive organisation, in order to convey to himself and to realise in his painting the actuality that is in front of him. To see the scene before his eyes demands a tremendous effort. We may say of the world of which we take note by a cursory glance or even an elementary description, that we do not really see it, thereby suggesting a perception which transcends in the sense of lying outwith the reach of everyday concern with that with which we are in contact.

We can after all distinguish perfectly well the elephants in a circus procession from those pink elephants mentioned by the headmistress of an English finishing school, when she said that a dutiful wife would never question her husband's word, even when he claimed to see such weird animals passing in colour before his eyes. But we would none of us ourselves think it likely that such husbands, however deferential their wives, perceived actual pink elephants. We all of us manage to distinguish perfectly well such entities (if they may be called entities), from elephants in the jungle, in the circus, at the zoo. Indeed, to borrow a phrase from David Hume, if we failed effectively to make such distinctions in our everyday commerce with the world around us, 'our lives would inevitably perish and go to ruin'. As Hume clearly recognised and as Kant in his much more formidably systematic style worked out, imagination (and for Kant understanding) were indeed in play in objective response to what our senses brought before us at the most rudimentary level. Yet when we come to reckon with Cézanne's experience we have to acknowledge perceptual experience which *transcends* our own, an experience which lies outwith our less achieved awareness. Thus we may speak of it significantly as expressive of a preoccupation with the transcendent. Indeed, we may go further and suggest that the obscure, many-sided, yet absolutely central notion of the transcendent, received a new, and possibly less baffling application from Cézanne's history.

Again, one must speak of the artist's commitment in terms which go beyond the idiom permitted to those who favour either a naturalistic reduction of our ethical concept, or who follow the alternative route of finding in our ethical language before all else a sort of method whereby we comment on human behaviour, stylise it, seek to modify it for good or for ill, to awaken in ourselves this or that response to this or that situation confronting us, but who deny it any factual import. We are here face to face with something absolute in a sense analogous to that of the claim of human nature to be treated as an end, and not as a means only. One could go further and suggest a commitment akin to that of Anselm's monks for whom he wrote his *Proslogion* when he found them deeply disturbed by the arguments of those who, like the fool in the Psalms, had said in their hearts that there is no God, seeking thus by their arguments to render his monks' consecration immune to such onslaughts and invulnerable to such criticism. Anselm did this by the attempt to exhibit the One to whom his monks' lives were committed as one whose existence it is in the end sheer self-contradiction to deny. His reality is for Anselm demonstrably involved as much in the possibility of internally self-consistent discourse for anyone who understood what he was saying as in the monastic life itself. Yet the situation to which Anselm's argument belonged, is constituted by his monks' dedication, and I would suggest that we may discern here something analogous to that which undoubtedly marked the life and the commitment of the painter.

So we meet here a very important paradox. There is something at first sight certainly scandalous to the empiricist if we take with the painter's seriousness what Cézanne would tell us concerning the structure of the perceptual. He forces upon our notice (the language may recall what Professor John Wisdom has said on many occasions) the easily neglected, often unnoticed richness and diversity of the everyday. In particular he may make us attend to the concrete particular and thereby effectively compel us to recognise the extent to which we arbitrarily restrict the sense of the familiar phrase 'our natural environment'. Alternatively we may, through a proper emphasis upon the complexity of sense-observation in its simpler forms, force upon our notice what we are continually taught to overlook. We may have forgotten (unless our field is physical optics, the physics of sound, and the physiology and psychology of perception) the need of attending to the very interior complexity of sense-perception itself, indeed of the most demanding experience which is the foundation of such perception. I said that there is something scandalous in Cézanne's preoccupation, to the dogmatic, or the nearly dogmatic, empiricist. But he may find himself compelled by this scandal to enlarge and deepen his very concept of experience, and of perceptual experience in particular. The positivist will very often wish to argue that to admit the reality of the external world is to do no more than to establish a set of rules for predicting the course of our sense-awareness, and to adhere to it as long as it is found reliable (the term predict is here used very loosely). In his brooding on perceptual experience, Cézanne echoes the experience of a heart set free for the full appreciation of what is suggested by the 'Analytic of Principles', and enabled to learn its lessons in concrete terms, thus substituting insight sprung from a multiplicity of examples for that which may be mediated by a general theory. Again the moralist must surely reckon with the problems posed for his confident generalisation by such examples of absolute dedication.

In a previous section of this book, I have argued that however difficult the structure of Plato's theory of forms (of the middle dialogues), however much attention must be paid to his engagement with a very complex philosophical and cosmological tradition that stood behind him, the theory is effectively to be seen as an attempt to reconstruct the order of being under the guiding impetus of a conviction that in the life and death of Socrates there was to be found a concretion, one might say a *mimēsis*, of the way in which things ultimately are. For Plato the life and death of Socrates could never be dismissed from the scheme of things as if tangential to its ultimate secrets. There is in the mood of speculation here briefly recapitulated a confident, if also a tentative, assumption that moral excellence achieved in and by an individual is properly taken as a point of departure (I have almost said *the* point of departure), for the revisionary metaphysician. This excellence is glimpsed as something unintelligible apart from the manner in which the man of whom it is predicated led his life. But what of the life of Cézanne, what of the artist's concentration? There is surely a sense in which recollection and admission of its reality as part of the furniture of the world in which we live must give pause not only to the philosophical claim (and here I must recall that Plato very nearly agreed with Bentham) that poetry is misrepresentation, but also to certain sorts of metaphysical construction, certain sorts of preoccupation with the transcendent. Thus, though in this long illustration I have continually insisted on the propriety of speaking of concern with the transcendent in connection with Cézanne's life, yet it is preoccupation with the transcendent in a different, although a comparable, sense to that which informs metaphysics and indeed to that which Plato saw as formative of Socrates' life and made the point of departure of his metaphysics. The preoccupation is analogous; so too the commitment. Such attention to this example not only liberates our conception of experience from the narrow styles in which it would be confined by the positivist; it also (if we are interested in the problem of metaphysics) liberates us from the bondage to an approach to that problem which speaks too narrowly in terms of a kind of generalised liberation from the positivist dogma.

Earlier in this book the metaphor of bondage and of liberation was used in connection with its central problem. It may be that some readers of this section will recall what was there said in the possibly tedious sketch of the positivist outlook from which we are now emerging. Yet, what I have been concerned to bring out here is that it is not only the positivist outlook which constitutes a sort of bondage; there may be a deeper bondage inflicted by the individual himself through wrong conception of the process of liberation; indeed here he may find himself confronted even though he does not know it with the threat of a more lasting imprisonment. In fact in this section we have made a transition from the problem of metaphysics to that of the metaphysician. What is the metaphysician about? What are his difficulties and his temptations? What are the errors to which he above all men is prone? His preoccupation with the transcendent may have been of such a kind that it hides the complex ramifications of the concept of transcendence from the grasp of his understanding. As I remarked a short time ago, the metaphysician's preoccupation may be expressive of a sort of intellectual extremism frighteningly akin to that of the positivist. Further, in that failing to recognise the ramifications of the transcendent he may turn himself from himself and moral blindness may quickly be born of a commitment mistaken in its Platonic concentration upon the one that stands over against the many. It is deeply significant that Bentham and Plato should have found themselves so nearly in agreement in dismissing poetry as misrepresentation, in finding in art at best a narrowly representative function. Thus, indeed both the Platonist and the positivist agree in dodging the disciplines of close attention to the concrete and familiar and the enlarged awareness of realities, and indeed of the way in which they reveal themselves to us that may be born of such piecemeal concentration.

Again, one is reminded of Goethe's dictum, borrowed by Coleridge, that we are all of us, if we philosophise at all, either a Platonist or an Aristotelian. In Platonic metaphysics, construction is expressive of response to a particular vision that the philosopher insists to be sovereign when perfectly achieved over all conceivable alternatives, if not exclusive of their modest claim. We have yet to come to terms in this book with the suggestion that the point of departure from which Plato moves towards this vision may compel a man to exercises in tragic, as distinct from Platonic, philosophical dialogue. It is indeed to that topic that we will shortly turn.

But before we do so it may be worth while to look again at the sort of transcendence to which we are introduced when deepening of perceptual experience enables us to go beyond our first simplicistic conception both of its objects and its internal structure. In a recent lecture, Professor R. V. Jones,[4] who now occupies Clerk-Maxwell's chair in the University of Aberdeen and who was much concerned in the war with the development and use of radar, remarked that the failure in February 1942 to note the passage into the English Channel of the German men-of-war, the *Scharnhorst* and the *Gneisenau*, may have been due to a failure on the part of highly trained observers, springing from prolonged intense concentration rather than from a momentary lapse of attention of the sort which a man is guilty of, when for instance, he turns from the area he is supposed to be observing through his telescope or from the radar screen which he is supposed to be closely watching momentarily to speak to his friends or to rest his eyes. Professor Jones was clearly concerned with a causal explanation that might belong to the psychology of perception; but such considerations raise important questions in the epistemological field where the frontiers of logical and causal enquiry are blurred, where indeed we are concerned with the conditions of effective observation, with the sorts of observation that may be powerful to reveal, and not by unnoticed aberration to conceal, what it is concerned with. The example again forces on our attention the complexity, the *internal* complexity of the perceptual experience, the sorts of discipline on which it depends. Here arguably in a much more restricted and specialised example we approach topics raised by Professor Polanyi in his criticism of the positivist philosophy of science. For Polanyi the positivist ignores the dimension of historical tradition, the way in which certain admittedly highly flexible and reformable standards of admissibility become part of the intellectual patrimony of those who enter the world of the laboratory in a free society. He is concerned with disciplines; they are disciplines transmitted socially, matters of *paideia* in the Greek sense, rather than

---

[4] The Lermour Lecture, delivered in Cambridge in the autumn of 1972.

brought to recognition by the sort of analysis of perceptual experience born of the work of Locke, Berkeley, Hume, Kant and their successors. What Professor Jones was referring to is an example that lies on the frontier of these two distinguishable emphases. He speaks of rules that might be formulated as part of a transmissible discipline; but these rules are based upon scrutiny of the deep, standing conditions of perceptual experience. In particular they raise questions concerning concentration, the way in which indeed in human life it may defeat itself.

It is with concentration in a more general and less restricted sense that we have been concerned in this chapter. If there is a unity in the field of its concern, in so far as its concern is with concentration, then that unity is found in the 'formal similarities' that various sorts of concentration make manifest, whether they are dismissed as restrictive, commended as deeply revealing, or fraught with the sort of ambivalence that demands correction. If the trained observers in Professor Jones' example, failed to notice what they had been schooled to look out for, they did so because they failed to sit back and allow the unexpected to intrude. It may be that that unexpected was totally unforeseeable in itself or only that sheer effort had numbed any readiness to respond to its sudden actuality. There is a paradox in speaking of learning to be ready for the unexpected. It is a paradox because the attitude is one that both positivist and metaphysical dogmatist find in different ways peculiarly uncongenial. And indeed we have to remember that a readiness to relish the unexpected for its own sake is one of the marks of the crank! Yet we have to allow for experiences to overtake us that shatter our frames of reference, or indeed vindicate those frames by showing that they give us the power to deal with just that unexpectedness, surrendering neither ourselves to it as if it were all-embracing revelation, nor belittling its significance by treating it as merely peripheral.

10

Miracle, irony, tragedy

In his Gifford Lectures, delivered before the University of Edinburgh in 1939 and 1940, Dr Reinhold Niebuhr remarked that the presence or absence of messianic expectation was one of the features most sharply differentiating one culture from another. One could regard such expectation as a variable for which, although the number of possible values is large, the range is in principle determinate. Niebuhr is surely right in saying that there are, as a matter of fact, both cultures and sub-cultures from which there is absent anything which could conceivably be regarded as satisfying the description 'messianic expectation'. Hitherto in this work we have been largely concerned with metaphysics as a *nisus* towards the transcendent, a *nisus ad extra*. But when we introduce the category of messianic expectation, we introduce, at least in principle, the idea of a movement *ab extra*. It is precisely this which the notion of miracle advertises in a way which remains extremely crude and unsophisticated, even when the conception of miraculous intervention has been rarefied and liberated from the most brashly anthropomorphic overtones or suggestions.

In the Christian tradition there is clearly discernible almost from the outset, an ambivalence in the presentation of the miraculous, where there is a self-conscious recognition that the concept is 'open-textured' and capable of the sort of enlargement that is ultimately hardly distinguishable from a radical transformation. To say this is not to suggest that there is a recognition of those features in the miraculous which men and women today find intellectually inadmissible, or morally intolerable. Thus, if a chemist refuses to admit the conversion of a large quantity of water into a corresponding amount of wine, because such a conversion involves a breach of universal chemical regularity, which he is not prepared to admit as possible, his refusal is grounded in his acceptance of certain natural regularities, unknown when the story of the marriage at Cana was first recounted, or set down; this acceptance is itself expressive of

114

his general adherence in the study of natural phenomena to certain procedures of inductive sampling which he regards as valid in principle, and which he is confident have been correctly applied in the case in question. The author of the Fourth Gospel was altogether ignorant of the fact that what he set down must be regarded as chemically impossible, and no exercise of a religiously sophisticated imagination will avail to bridge the gulf between his contemporaries and ours, where this matter is concerned.

Again, there is only a very faint yet possibly traceable discernment of a problem which certainly men and women today find to press hard upon them. The question is immediately posed to the morally sensitive conscience why certain individuals should be selected as the beneficiaries of some sort of miraculous intervention. If we suppose that such interventions do, as a matter of fact, take place, we cannot but ask how it comes about that certain individuals, and not others, all alike involved in situations of great human need, are singled out for special treatment. I mean the sort of special treatment which was denied to the Jews in Europe during the years of their recent hardly paralleled suffering, still vivid in the memory and imagination of the world. Their cry for deliverance went, for the most part, unanswered. To these issues I shall return later in the section of this work touching on the complex of issues known as the 'problem of evil'. For the present I would simply emphasise that, although there is faintly discernible an acknowledgement of the reality of this latter problem in the Christian tradition, it is only faintly discernible.

Yet, when these points have been made, and indeed after they have been developed at a greater length than this chapter allows, we have to reckon that within the Christian tradition there is a curious, indeed impressive edginess over the kind of claim which may be based on an admission of the allegedly miraculous powers of Jesus. Here, to make my point, I shall develop one crucially important example. The writer of the Fourth Gospel certainly believed that Jesus had raised Lazarus from the dead, whether or not it is a matter of historical fact that he did so, and that his success in doing this, four days after Lazarus had died, when corruption had already set in, provided the occasion on which his enemies decided that they must make an end of him, and of Lazarus also, in that his continual presence among men was bound to be intensely disturbing. So Caiaphas gave counsel that it was expedient that 'one man should die for the people'. The account of the meeting of the Sanhedrin is absolutely clear, and sharply penetrating in the way in which the author captures the mentality of the responsible ecclesiastical statesman, concerned to preserve institutional structures against the threat to which they were unquestionably exposed by the encouragement of extravagant religious zeal. In less than forty years after the events in question allegedly took place, the Romans did indeed come and lay bare the place and nation of which Caiaphas believed himself the responsible warden. Whatever the factual truth or falsity of the story of Lazarus, the response of the authorities is unquestionably true to human reality. It is a mistake indeed to suggest that the attitude of mind expressed in the counsel that one man should die lest the whole nation perish, is altogether morally intolerable. The language is that which the responsible statesman must use: it is indeed part of his burden and his tragedy that it falls to him on occasion to give just such advice, not in order to secure his own personal position, but to fulfil the harsh load of responsibility which he carries. Indeed, he has to cultivate a certain detachment, even a remoteness from the individual who is exposed to the consequences of his decision, in order that firmness of purpose shall not be imperilled by an intrusive sentiment.

Yet there is more to be said. In the first part of this work I referred to Plato's continually illuminating myth of Gyges. In that myth what gave Gyges his immunity from personal danger in violation of the sanctions whereby conventional morality is safeguarded, was his ability to turn himself invisible. It was this power which he obtained by the fortunate discovery of the magical ring, that enabled him to transgress traditional morality with immunity. So he was a man with whom it was far from safe for others to meddle! One might have thought that a man who had proved himself capable of recalling even one corpse to life, was even more dangerous to meddle with, that such a one was, in principle at least, altogether invulnerable; for it is hard imaginatively to conceive a personal sovereignty in practical life more absolute than one exercised within the tomb. Yet, in the story as we have it from the pen of a writer who always displayed a remarkable capacity, even a virtuosity, in organising his material to secure the maximum effect, Caiaphas is depicted as altogether unafraid, quite confident that what he deemed desirable, namely the extermination of a man whom he judged a sort of public danger, could be easily accomplished. This may seem a small point; but I would suggest that in a work as subtly organised as the Fourth Gospel unquestionably is, it is surely worth noticing that the one who is presented as able to raise a dead man to life, is within the context of the same episode, treated as in principle destructible, as indeed highly vulnerable to decisive, carefully prepared action. If we treat the raising of Lazarus as an event which somehow focusses and gathers to a point what is presented in this narrative as supremely disturbing, in Jesus we have to admit the paradox that his enemies see deep enough, or are presented as seeing deep enough, to realise that it is a sheer mistake to infer from this that he is indestructible. He must be destroyed; so his enemies decide, and their decision is not vacuous because its implementation is possible.

In this chapter my concern is with the topic of the relation of the transcendent, of which we say that it enters miracle stories as their subject, with the transcendent of the metaphysicians' concern. We have always represented the speculative or revisionary metaphysician as moving from the relative to the ultimate, from the finite to the infinite, from the limited to the absolute. In such a miracle story as the one with which we are concerned, it is in several respects quite different. Thus we do not leave, as it were, the relative behind us. Lazarus is presented as a man whose life will go on, and who will die a second time, on this occasion presumably to remain in the tomb until the process of corruption is complete, and his bones moulder. Again we cannot escape the similarities between this story and the tale, for instance, of Heracles' rescue of Alcestis. It is the tale of a mighty act of unprecedented power that intrudes upon the ordinary routines of human life; almost one is tempted to say that here one finds omnipotence depressed to the measure of a tale that is told, found expressed in the supremely magnified powers of a man like ourselves, destroying temporarily the rhythms of ordinary life, which then resume their course. But what is crucial in the narrative is that this resumption touches not the beneficiary of Jesus' power alone, but himself supremely. Nothing can be the same again for Jesus; yet while his foes take every care to compass his arrest discreetly, he is so ordinary that it would seem that the services of the mercenary traitor were partly to finger out this very ordinary man, when the light of torches and lanterns hardly availed clearly to distinguish one who had previously eluded stoning for blasphemy by the simple device of mingling with the temple crowd and escaping (John 8). This thing was done to prepare the way for the supreme manifestation of divine power in Jesus, namely the laying down of his life. His enemies are right to see that the circumstances of his miraculous act do not contradict, but rather indicate, his ordinariness and consequent vulnerability. So we have to do with a manifestation of omnipotence, which precipitates a decision taken by a man in a position of great responsibility, to eliminate the one in whom the omnipotence is disclosed, which is described almost in terms of naturalistic realism.

I am fully aware how great are the historical problems which arise at this point, how great, indeed, are those other questions concerning causality to which I made reference earlier in this chapter. But it seems legitimate temporarily to avert attention from such problems and to attend to the peculiar interweaving in the Lazarus narrative of the mysterious and the familiar. What follows may seem curiously naive; but on occasion one must not shrink from the appearance of naivety if one is to advance one's understanding of a concept. In traditional metaphysical theism, God is represented as omnipresent, omniscient, omnipotent; he is also referred to as simple in the technical sense that in him those attributes coincide with himself, and in another sense coincide one with another. That is, of course, in so far as they are predicable of God, as he is in himself. No passage in the writings of Thomas Aquinas is more often quoted today than the one in which, speaking of natural knowledge of God, he says that of God we know that he is, what he is not, and what relation everything other than himself has to him. The very healthy agnosticism of that passage is rightly emphasised, and it may well be claimed that when we speak of omnipresence, omniscience, omnipotence, we are indeed speaking, not of God, but of the relation to him of that which falls outside his being, its relation or, more accurately, discriminable aspects of its fundamental dependence. Where omnipotence in particular is concerned, we may be familiar with some, at least, of the historical controversies associated with the notion. One might take as an example the problem familiar to any student of Descartes, of God's relation to the eternal truths of which he is regarded by that philosopher as the author or creator.

There is, however, and here I repeat I am being deliberately naive, even childish, where the notion of omnipotence is concerned, a curious oscillation between what I can only call cosmological and ethical interest. To refer again to Niebuhr's Gifford Lectures, when he spoke of divine transcendence he did so in a way that showed that for him it was very closely linked with omnipotence as he understood it. In his fundamental theology at this point, he is quite unselfconsciously anthropomorphic, and indeed he identifies God's transcendence with his non-involvement in the actual destiny of his creation and consequent freedom to take new initiatives in history. It is, for him, the ground of a kind of limitless resourcefulness which he seems to attribute to God in exercise of effectively sovereign control over the whole of human history. I repeat the language is anthropomorphic, and it may be that from Niebuhr's self-indulgence at this point we learn, in a very clear example, something of the urgent need in which the theologian stands of the services of the metaphysician, if he is to avoid the ultimately destructive paradox of anthropomorphism. Niebuhr, indeed, is betrayed by the strength of his prophetic passion into justifying such self-indulgence on the grounds that the vision by which he is engaged is altogether beyond the reach of discursive rationality. Yet, even though his view demands rigorous criticism, Niebuhr advertises the extent to which, in the analysis of the notion of omnipotence one must discipline oneself to think, not only cosmologically, but also ethically. In referring to Niebuhr's view, I spoke of his representing God as exercising effectively sovereign control over the whole of human history. The word 'sovereign' was not used accidentally, and a moment's attention to its use here suggests that the employment is by no means alien from that which one meets in familiar classics of political theory and political science. Where there is sovereign power, whether executive or legislative, there we have to reckon with a power bound by nothing outside itself in its disposition of those matters which fall within its concern. No man or institution orders to the sovereign the way in which that sovereign conducts its affairs, owing allegiance to none, its supremacy being focussed in its unfettered control of its own comings and goings. So political theorists and scientists speak of the sovereign's 'omnipotence', and in his understanding of divine sovereignty it is this omnipotence which Niebuhr has extrapolated. When such a theologian as Niebuhr predicates sovereignty analogically of God, he means that none outside himself orders the ways of his going. His word is final. It is for this reason that Niebuhr's treatment is correctly interpreted as emphasising the ethical over against the cosmological dimensions of the notion.

To return now to the story from the Gospel according to St John we may say again that part, at least, of what the writer has asked his readers to find in the narrative is a manifestation of omnipotence *in concreto*. This manifestation is dramatically decisive in that here the very frontiers of human life are revealed as subdued to the feat of the central figure of the story. Of course, the author seems, and this is brought out very well in the contrast between the way Lazarus emerges from the charnel house, and the condition in which the tomb of Christ himself is later discovered, to emphasise the contrast between the relativity of Lazarus' deliverance, and the finality of Christ's resurrection. Yet still it is with a manifestation of omnipotence that we must reckon, a manifestation occasioned in the very complex narrative by various circumstances and motives, a revelation to the disciples of the glory of God, but also of the love, whatever that word here may mean, borne by the central figure to his friend. Yet (I repeat), it is as a manifestation of omnipotence *in concreto* that it is presented. Immediately the omnipotence is thus decisively manifested, a question-mark is set against the way in which we must easily understand it. It is almost as if the writer (who is a supreme ironist), is ironically reminding his readers that very soon they will realise if they follow the story to the end, that this is not 'the real thing'. Rather it is an episode that must take place in order that the substance, as distinct from the shadow of divine omnipotence, may be shown. The way in which, if we think ethically in Niebuhr's sense, we schematise the concept of divine omnipotence, is too closely in bondage to associations borrowed from the world of sovereign power, the world of Caesar's *imperium*. We are confronted in the story with the actuality of dominion over the frontiers of death. Our sense of what such dominion must be may be overlaid by memories of an authority at once arbitrary and absolute, which is imperious in the manner in which it brooks no competitor to its own untrammelled sway; we think of Lazarus' raising not as the Father's answer to Jesus' prayer, but a crude manifestation of sovereignty shown *in concreto* to be thereby limitless and invincible. Yet John's narrative urges on our attention the paradox that such thinking belongs to the world of myth, almost of fairy-tale. The reality is quite different; it is found in a bitter submission to the harsh realities of human life, an exposure of the ethical substance of the human scene that goes far beyond, at once in its familiarity and its strangeness, the power exercised at the grave of Lazarus.

So the concept of a transcendent, miraculous intervention is employed in this story with simple emphasis, and indeed unfaltering directness. Yet as soon as it is so employed, or even before the deployment is complete (if one attends to the intricacies of the narrative), it is radically criticised. The criticism is not that of the logically sophisticated metaphysician; still less is it that of the modern who is deeply sensitive to causal impossibilities. Rather the mood of the criticism is ironic; the reader is encouraged almost to laugh at his

natural impulse to take the narrative with an utter and final seriousness, or else to dismiss it as a tale that is told him. The dismissal is
immanent in the narrative itself; yet it is a strange dismissal, which
takes the shape of converting the narrative into an account of preparation for the achievement of its own radical criticism. If we are to
approach *in concreto* the stuff of omnipotence, we must do it this
way. We must perceive the thing in its strangeness, in order to
school ourselves to grasp its ultimate reality in the desperately familiar. Almost we must learn to make the strange into the merely (but
emphatically not quite) trivial, in order to approach the unutterable
profundities of the familiar, in order to learn to see that familiar
anew, as indeed finding at its own level, but not out of its own
resources, the means of its transformation.

11

The transcendence of the tragic

Sophocles concludes *The Women of Trachis* with the following lines, spoken by Hyllus:

> You see how little compassion the Gods
> have shown in all that's happened; they
> who are called our fathers, who begot us,
> can look upon such suffering.
> No one can foresee what is to come.
> What is here now is pitiful for us
> and shameful for the Gods;
> But of all men it is hardest for him
> who is the victim of this disaster.
> Maiden, come from the house with us.
> You have seen a terrible death
> and agonies, many and strange, and there is
> nothing here which is not Zeus.

The Women of Trachis is a strange, indeed a formidable, play. Its action has its origin in events that are at once extreme and trivial and are also imbued with a crude supernaturalism that creates an immediate barrier for the modern spectator or reader. Yet, Ezra Pound occupied part of his time in captivity completing a new and very striking translation of the Greek original on the ground that this Sophoclean tragedy represented the very highest achievement of Greek literature. None the less, apart altogether from the crude supernaturalism mentioned above, the play seems to fall into two parts, with the suture between them inserted in a way that seems artificial and arbitrary. The episode of the shirt of Nessus ends with the realisation of Heracles that he has been mortally injured by the poison with which his wife's gift was impregnated, and with Deianira's suicide when she realises that her efforts to regain her husband's affection have not only failed but occasioned his death, and that the air is ringing with the curses he has called down upon her head for doing so. The second part of the play is concerned with Heracles' death upon the great funeral pyre which he bids his son, Hyllus, build. In an essay on this play in a volume devoted to Sophoclean tragedy, the French scholar, M. Georges Méautis, suggested that we find in this concluding section of the drama the presentation of the hero's apotheosis purified by suffering and admitted to the company of the immortals. Méautis' whole study suffers from an apologetic eagerness to find Christian themes in Sophoclean tragedies. To suggest that in Heracles' last hours he is purified by suffering endured as in the traditional Christian presentation that of Christ upon the cross was endured is to forget that the hero continues to curse his wife to the last, and that if we are to find analogies here with Christ's passion, we must represent Jesus as calling down the wrath of Heaven upon his executioners, demanding that they shall be consumed in the fires of Hell, not forgiven as men who know not what they do. Certainly Hyllus' marriage with the unhappy Iole is artificial and induces a sense of contrived unreality. But the concluding lines of the tragedy which I have quoted at the beginning of this chapter bind both its sections into a discernible unity. The last lines proclaim the inscrutability of Heaven, laying upon Zeus the monstrous event in which the gentle Deianira has been engulfed.

There are, of course, other tragedies of Sophocles, in particular the *Antigone*, which speak of a world far less remote from ours than this strange society of semi-divine heroes as little subject to normal human limitation in their lust as in the scope of their achievements, of monstrous centaurs, and the rest. In the *Trachiniae* we move in a world indifferent to natural constants as it is always seemingly indifferent to moral distinctions, and always fraught with the terrors of the unknown and the uncontrollable, inscrutable *fiat* of Heaven. Moreover, in the *Antigone*, its heroine, by the manner of her death, seems to achieve a sort of victory over the forces that would destroy her. Her brusque dismissal of Haemon's claims, the incomprehension with which in their first encounter she confronts her uncle, Creon, still at that time ready to give real consideration to his people's right to be heard in affairs of state, the recognisably incestuous character of her preoccupation with the memory of her unburied brother, the amazonian quality of her treatment of her sister, Ismene – all these inescapable and potentially destructive flaws in her nature are subdued by the manner of her going to her death.[1] Yet, where her uncle

---

[1] I owe much to the treatment of this play by André Bonnard in his book, *L'Homme et la tragédie* (La Baconnière, Centre du Livre Suisse, 1949–50).

is concerned, these flaws have been more than potentially destructive. Certainly, one must reject Hegel's interpretation of the play as the presentation of a conflict between two systems of right, one represented by Creon and the other by Antigone. There is no doubt that for the author Antigone is defending a higher cause than her uncle. Yet, her confrontation with her uncle, while it is not by itself a sufficient necessary condition for the actualisation of his destructive self-obsession and his identification of the order of the *polis* with his own personal dignity, still remains in the action of the play the trigger which releases Creon's fury. Even as Deianira, by her gentleness and surely forgivable folly in her use of the centaur's gift, precipitates her husband's hatred, thrusting him to death in unforgiving resentment against his wife, so Antigone cannot be regarded as herself altogether innocent of the disastrous consequences flowing from her care of the 'unwritten laws'.

It is often said that, where the Christian religion is concerned, those who accept its claim and seek to practise it, have moved beyond tragedy. Yet, one could claim that where the treatment of 'the problem of evil' is concerned, we reach an area in which in very various ways, theologians have allowed apologetic eagerness to lead them to suppose they had reached solutions, when in fact they had hardly begun effectively to articulate their problems – this, though great constructive energy has been devoted to resolve in one way or another questions raised by the ontological status of evil, whether physical and moral, by the seeming divine permission of the continuance of the humanly intolerable (always subtly distinguished from positive willing that things should be so), by the nature of suffering and the role both of physical suffering and the endurance of spiritual injury issuing from the moral obliquity of stress in human perfecting, etc. It would be both philistine and arrogant to belittle such efforts or to fail at least to extract from them insights significant in respect of this or that problem.

Thus Teilhard de Chardin, in his letters, wrote with deep insight of the nature and the role in human life, of that gradual, besetting diminution of human energies, which often reaches a harrowing term in senility and related conditions. Certainly in letters which are in part letters of spiritual direction, he suggests ways in which the substitution in the inevitable process of human ageing, of passive for active response to circumstances, may be accepted and converted into a school of spiritual advance. But the alleged general solution of 'the problem of evil', the all-inclusive answer to the questions elicited by bitter experience of suffering, whether through illness, natural disaster, or by consequence of the wicked actions of others over whose purposes one has no control is something of a different order. In the Scriptures of the Old Testament, the Book of Job (in which some commentators have, probably mistakenly but none the less understandably, found analogies with the tragic drama of the Greeks) remains as a standing protest against the suggestion that undeserved suffering can find through the intellectual virtuosity and consecrated zeal of the apologist a justification which will still in the sufferer the sense of outrage that must remain. In the chapter which was devoted to the relation of the transcendent to the miraculous, it was suggested that where, for instance, the presentation of Christ's sufferings in the Gospel according to St John was concerned, the transcendent import of these events was suggested by the masterly use of such devices as *double-entendre* and in particular a devastating irony. It was hinted rather than expressly stated that this irony has an unmistakably tragic quality. Certainly the writer succeeded in suggesting that where the supreme events were concerned, the 'sign' of the lifting up of the Son of Man from the earth, we have to reckon with an action whose transcendent significance demands that its presentation shall be freed from any suggestion of the portentous, any hint of the momentary penetration of its darkness by light eloquent of a divine concern – this without allowing the reader to forget that it is a tale of disaster. The Roman procurator, in his angry resentment against those whom he supposed to have blackmailed him into connivance with their purpose, is constrained to witness, in spite of his personal capitulation from fear of Tiberius' anger to the Jewish priests, to the kingship of the man whom he thus abandoned to death: 'What I have written I have written.' It is those who are represented as translating into the idiom of public clamour the principles implicit in Caiaphas' ecclesiastical statesmanship, who cry, 'We have no king but Caesar.' Inevitably, the reader's mind is flooded with memories of the ancient record, recalling Israel's hesitation, even hostility, *vis-à-vis* the very institution of that kingship of which Saul was the first exemplar, David the second – this because such institution might create a barrier between Yahweh's people and their God. If irony is used here, it is a tragic irony. And indeed, if one turns from John's record to other earlier versions of the same event, the presence within them, as they are realised in the evangelists' imagination, of a deeply tragic quality, becomes quite unmistakable.

An emotional woman once remarked to the great Duke of Wellington that a victory must surely be one of the most wonderful of life's experiences, something full of a hardly imaginable exhilaration and sense of achievement. The Duke, who was after all many times a victorious commander in the field, replied, 'Madam, a victory is the most tragic thing in the world, only excepting a defeat.' No doubt he was thinking in the first instance of the bitter physical suffering inevitably endured by those whose captain he had often been in gaining the success in question.[2] But we can surely suppose that he was also vividly aware of the problems of reconciliation that were almost inevitably made more intractable by infliction of necessity upon the enemy of the bitterness of defeat upon the field of battle. During the Spanish Civil War of 1936-9, the late Sir Winston Churchill is alleged to have remarked that, 'the more merciful will win this war; grass grows on battlefields but never on the site of scaffolds'.[3] Certainly Churchill was right to recognise that where civil war, in which brother has fought against brother, is concerned, the bitterness inevitable after victory is exacerbated, the work of reconciliation almost impossibly hard.

It is characteristic of traditional Christian devotion, whether public or private, to acclaim Christ as victor, and indeed, such language pervades the New Testament Scriptures. In the Fourth Gospel, in his last conversations with his disciples, Jesus warns them of the suffering that will be their lot, but seeks to strengthen their will to endure it by affirming that he has overcome the world in which that suffering will overtake them. Again, in Paul's letter to the Romans Christ is acclaimed as the one who has given his followers victory, that indeed over him in the endless life into which he has entered death has no more sovereignty, that by him the last enemy, death itself, will be destroyed. The language is highly metaphorical and its sense obscure; for while we can remotely perhaps conceive a life that is not bounded by the frontier of death, that is no matter of coming to be and passing away, we are defeated in any attempt to make our own the sense of language speaking of the destruction, even the death, of death.

Yet, at a more easily assimilable level, particularly in the Gospel according to St Luke (a subject of particular interest for contemporary professional students of the New Testament), Jesus is presented as in his passion victoriously enduring a prolonged and

---

[2] Anaesthesia, and effective antiseptic medication, lay in the future in 1815.
[3] One can hardly claim this prophecy (if intended as that) was fulfilled.

supremely searching temptation. At the end of the tale of his tempting in the desert, when he has rejected the climactic suggestion that
he cast himself from the pinnacle of the temple with a passionate
affirmation of the law, 'Thou shalt not put God to the test', it is
stated that the devil leaves him *achri kairou*. The *kairos* in question
would seem to be the hour of 'the power of darkness' which comes
upon him when the devil enters into Judas Iscariot, tempting the
latter to betray his master to his foes. It is true that in the upper
room he speaks of his disciples as 'those who have continued with
me in my temptations'; but the word translated 'temptations' would
seem there to refer not to the ordeal in the desert nor to the supreme
ordeal for which the former was a preparation, but to the daily pressures so likely to deflect Jesus from his ministry and to disturb
and disorientate him in his mission. In the final Satanic tempting his
disciples will be put to the test, Peter, especially, sifted like wheat,
tried and found wanting, yet arguably able through the self-
knowledge won through frantic failure of nerve, when he has come
to himself, to strengthen his brethren.

Certainly Luke presents Jesus tempted to the uttermost, yet
remaining without sin, victorious, and at last, the ordeal over, in a
kind of muted triumph, committing his spirit to his Father. It is
often remarked by modern students of Luke's Gospel and its supposed sequel or second volume, the Acts of the Apostles, that leaving
on one side the special problems raised by the birth stories, we are
offered the narrative of a triumphal progress. Rejected at the outset
in his home town of Nazareth, Jesus moves to Galilee and then, his
Galilean ministry over, he moves in a kind of triumphal progress to
Jerusalem. In Jerusalem he dies; but his death is little more than a
momentary eclipse, the matter of an hour in which the powers of
darkness seem to prevail, to be followed by his rising. Then, at the
beginning of the book of the Acts, after a second rehearsal of the
Ascension which brought the appearances of the risen Jesus to an
end, we have the strange tale of the events of the following Pentecost
at Jerusalem foreshadowing indeed the confession of Jesus' name by
men of all nations in the Mediterranean world which will be accomplished as, following a series of checks at Jerusalem and in the
surrounding country the progress is resumed, with Paul, converted
on the Damascus way, its principal agent, turning to the Gentiles
and inevitably finding his way by stages to Rome. Certainly, the
book of the Acts is a work of vastly inferior theological insight and
indeed of far less intellectually rigorous discipline in organisation of

its often fascinating material than the Gospel which preceded it. Indeed, the differences in depth of insight (illustrated in a devastating way by the horrifying story of Ananias and Sapphira) are so great that one who is in no sense a specialist in the field of New Testament study can understand why there have been critics who have sought to attribute the Acts to another hand than that of the author of the Gospel. But we are not concerned with these admittedly important issues, except in so far as the design of the later work has encouraged a certain willingness to overlook the deep complexity of the Gospel. To suggest that we are presented with a developing ministry success-fully achieved in consequence of superficial failure, the latter swallowed up by its obliteration in the progress that it makes possible, is a travesty of the book's disturbing and complex reality.

Thus, when the alleged triumphal progress to Jerusalem is nearing its end and Jesus beholds the city, he weeps over it, his words expres-sive of an overwhelming sense of futility and defeat. Again, at the very outset, if the term of his journey is characterised as an assump-tion (the Greek *analēmpsis*), yet still in preparation for it he must set his face steadfastly 'to go to Jerusalem'; and in the Greek the aorist *estērixen*, used to indicate that resolution belongs to the verb whose perfect passive is used in the parable of Dives and Lazarus to indicate the gulf between Heaven and Hell. Further, it is often re-marked that whereas in Mark's version Jesus dies alone and uncomforted, in Luke women of Jerusalem mourn for him as he bears his cross. But are they thanked? Rather, they are addressed in words resonant both of the lament over the city and of his rebuff to the sentimental woman who blessed the womb that bore him and the breasts at which he was suckled. It is in language fusing the attitudes expressed on these two very different occasions that they are bidden, 'Weep not for me but for yourselves' – this because of the disasters he foresaw must overtake the city to which he had journeyed in little more than thirty years' time. Any possibility of his contributing by word or action to help avoid such final catas-trophe was gone. His mission had ended in disaster. But of course these considerations only take us to the circumference of the tragic reality.

Earlier in this chapter, a glancing reference was made to the Book of Job. It is not unknown for commentators on the epistle to the Romans to point to a certain similarity between the style and temper of the two works. This comes in the second part where the convert Paul engages with the problem set him by the breach between the community to which he now belongs and the Israel in whose traditions he had been schooled. The extent to which the teaching of this letter has been invoked in the bitter dogmatic controversies of later centuries particularly obscures its character as the argument of a man seeking to find sense in a bitterly destructive schism that he has experienced in himself and in the external world, whose bitterness he has continually 'proved on his pulses'. One might even say that where the writers of the Gospels are concerned, they also are in different ways engaged by 'the problem of evil', seeking not to answer it in general terms but somehow or other to assimilate the devastating concrete reality which focussed its issues for them, namely the rejection of the one they believed to be the Messiah by the people to whom he came. The most devastating intellectual and spiritual temptation to which indeed some of them (and I am thinking especially of the Luke of the book of the Acts) yielded was that of presenting the catastrophic course of events as expressive of the working of a traceable providential order. So, in the events that led to the execution of Jesus, the role of the Jewish authorities is painted in darker colours and that of the Roman procurator and his officers gradually limited to that of the unwilling executance of a nefarious design, compelled by the circumstances of official function to play the parts to which the guile of those ultimately responsible constrained them. What actually happened, the way in which responsibility should in fact be distributed, remains at present obscure. But what is clear is the emergence of an apologetic style which seeks to make the intolerable bearable, even edifying, which seeks also to eliminate the element of unfathomable mystery by the attempt to move beyond tragedy. So, in ways too sadly familiar across the centuries, the Christian apologetic has found for instance in the Pax Augusta the divinely ordered setting for the advance of the Gospel in spite of the fierce resistance of the Jewish authorities. In almost every place in which it is preached Rome allows its message to be heard. The historical reality of the Roman imperial system comes to be lost in a golden light that allows the student only to remember for instance the extent to which, following the special command given to Pompeius against the pirates under the Lex Gabinia, the power of Rome protected travellers against the threat of such interference with their journeying and thus helped to make possible the complex travels of the missionary Paul. But the student of Roman history can neither forget the order thus established, the threat of lawless villainy thus contained, nor the means whereby such law was imposed and upheld. Even the reader whose knowledge of Octavian's struggle for supremacy in the Roman world is limited to Shakespeare's presentation of the young man in his Roman tragedies, can hardly forget altogether the means the architect of the Pax Augusta was prepared to use in order to establish himself in a position of unchallengeable mastery. One thinks of his active complicity as a very young man in the liquidation of the representatives of the old order by proscription. If Hegel is criticised for the glibness with which he identifies dialectically the ideal with the actual, we must not forget the extent to which the inspiration of his argument can be found in the history of the Christian religion on which that formidable metaphysician had long brooded.

The events of the present century and in particular what happened in Germany between 1933 and 1945 rob any serious theologian of the remotest excuse for ignoring the tragic element in Christianity. It was in the long Christian centuries and by the styles of persistent Christian behaviour that the ground was prepared for the acceptance of the holocaust of the Jewish people. I am not speaking of connivance, let alone actual participation in the running of the trains that carried thousands of ordinary men and women to Auschwitz; I am rather referring to a blunting of the sensibility which inhibited men and women from any sort of effective intervention until it was too late and all was over. The failure of Pope Pius XII drastically to intervene (even if his efforts had proved totally unavailing) on behalf of the Jews of Rome is often mentioned. But in the context of the present argument, emphasis for purposes of illustration might more effectively fall on a work published in Germany in 1934 by the great New Testament scholar, the late Professor Gerhard Kittel, *Die Judenfrage*. Kittel's name is best known to students of the New Testament as the first editor of the famous New Testament wordbook; his reputation as a scholar was already well established when he bent the energies of his mind and the resources of his scholarly understanding to the preparation of this essay in which he offered in 1934 an allegedly theological apologia for the kind of treatment which at that stage of the Nazi revolution was being meted out to the Jewish population. The reader of the work has to remember the context of its publication; if he does, he may well find its argument more deeply shocking than the obscene pornography associated with the name of the late Julius Streicher. But were Kittel alive to defend himself, he might claim that he had done little more than to bring up to date strands of thought discernible in parts of that very New

Testament itself, of which indeed he was himself a distinguished student.

The direction of this argument may seem momentarily obscure; certainly the time has come to rejoin the more direct attempt to recapture the tragic element in the Christian vision with which it was initially concerned. The remark of the Duke of Wellington concerning the character of a victory, as the most tragic thing in the world, only excluding a defeat, abundantly applies to Christ's victory. He made his choices, believing that they were in accordance with his Father's will. In Luke's account of his temptation in the wilderness, the climax is reached not with the offer of the kingdoms of this world and the glory of them, but with the suggestion that he should, by a dramatic descent from the pinnacle of the temple, at once establish beyond question in his own mind the reality of the powers at his disposal and by their exercise in this overwhelmingly self-assertive act establish himself as a force to be reckoned with where the destiny of his people was concerned. He refuses the suggestion that he should thus put his Father to the test in an action whereby at the same time, if it were successfully executed, he would impose his own sense of his mission upon his people. By his refusal he rejects not only any attempt to achieve success by use of political power, but the subtler, arguably deadlier temptation of a bloodless victory whereby he might establish himself as the leader of a great spiritual revival or what you will. So it is that by the same refusal by which he maintains obedience to his Father, he keeps himself free to be the open associate of tax-gatherers and harlots, of all on the very fringes of respectable society or beyond its boundaries. There is something almost ruthless in the way in which Luke emphasises Jesus' seeming preference for the disreputable and the worthless. (Among other examples of such an emphasis one may recall the references in material that is peculiar to him, to Samaritans, the implication of the parables of the two brothers and of the Pharisee and the tax-gatherer, the haunting story of his anointing in the house of Simon the Pharisee, etc.) There is no other work in the New Testament which is more nearly antinomian in its suggestion; but the context in which this behaviour by the central figure is set is a context provided by his initial choice, and the stern resolution by which it is continued.[4]

---

[4] It is strange that the Luke who thus in his Gospel flirts with anti-nomianism has so little to say in Acts on the issues on which Paul fought, concerning Gentile converts, obligations to the Jewish Law and the deeper issues of law and grace.

It is in the story of the crucifixion that this emphasis receives its final definition. Arguably, on one view of the text, the weight is made to fall almost entirely on the challenge to the crucified to prove himself Messiah by a dramatic descent from the cross. The dialogue between the two robbers crucified with him finds its setting in this angry debate, the challenge by the one that Jesus save himself and the two hanging beside him, taking up the cry of those around his gallows. It is impossible for anyone reading Luke's narrative as a work of literature not to catch here again the substance of the final challenge in the desert to cast himself from the pinnacle of the temple. In the renewal of his temptation by the devil, it is pre-eminently the final temptation that is renewed, with the clear implication that if he yields (as clearly the author supposes he might have done) his action will, by reason of its appalling circumstances, have an effect greater than the imagination can easily compass. But of course such a response would inevitably withdraw him from the situation in which he may receive the strange confession of faith of the other thief, and respond to it by the elusive, perplexing promise by which it was answered. Yet his continuing in a place that makes such intimate exchange possible is also the perfection of his obedience to his Father. Thus, the terrible episode concludes with his commendation of his soul to that Father, echoing the almost proud rejection in the refusal of the temptation to put his Father to the test. Finally, the centurion confesses him a just man and it is possible the justice there attributed to him is the justice of the wholly innocent, the justice that in the parable of the Pharisee and the tax-gatherer was in fact attributable neither to the one nor to the other, the tax-gatherer only by virtue of his penitence going down to his house acquitted of guilt at the bar of the divine scrutiny by reason of the depth of his self-knowledge and confidence in a divine mercy.

We are not concerned here (as we have been in an earlier chapter) even with aspects of the problem of miracle. It is enough to allow that Luke supposed miracles to be possible, as it is clear beyond shadow of question that he did. The possibility of Jesus' extricating himself by a totally overwhelming gesture from a predicament in which he was caught is a presupposition of his narrative. He makes it plain that this possibility was rejected. Indeed, the curious reference to Herod's hope to see a miracle done by Jesus suggests that he did, in the context of this terrible climax of his tale, dismiss with a a sort of disdain the suggestion that Herod's hope might have been fulfilled. This indeed is impressive, especially when one recalls the extent to which in his second volume Luke presents the apostles as indulging from time to time in exercises of the crudest sort of thaumaturgy. One might almost say that in the deepest sense in Jesus' supreme hour, miracle is ethically out of place. There is no attempt to substitute an effort to bring out the transcendent implications of his tale, the tragic irony which John employs to such effect. The narrative remains direct. Yet the reader is arguably only enabled to grasp what is being said if he carries with him a clear memory of what has gone before, thus enabling himself to discern the organisation of the whole book. If the reader makes this effort then he finds himself again thrust up against a deeply tragic reality. Jesus' response to temptation is unquestionably victory; that is attested by the centurion's proclamation of his innocence. Yet, as we have seen, it is victory achieved at an appalling cost, indeed at the cost of irretrievable defeat in that city in which, in Jesus' own words, 'a prophet must perish'. The ambiguity remains, an ambiguity from which, through the false comfort provided by a crude apologetic, the Christian Church has continually turned away. Indeed, one could claim that in Luke's second volume, one finds quite unmistakable signs of this sort of intellectual, indeed spiritual, apostasy. It may be indeed that if a writer seeks, as Luke did, to trace the advance of the Christian Church in its missionary work, he will always, if he is attempting to present the theme as a theologian and not with the cool detachment of a modern secular historian, present the events he describes as falling into a pattern that he will render ultimately edifying at whatever cost in over-simplification and downright misrepresentation of actuality. It is not only that Luke dulls the bitterness of the sorts of conflict that came near to tearing the early church apart; rather it is that he presents every circumstance that contributed to the manner of its progress as somehow providentially ordered to secure an advance divinely ordained and therefore in respect of all that made its progress possible, however morally ambiguous, something divinely permitted. It may be that he was betrayed into this forgetfulness of the profundities to which he felt his way in his first volume by his own identification with the institution whose history he traced. In his first volume he was not dealing with the progress of an institution which he himself sought to serve and through that service find a role for himself under Heaven. Rather he was presenting a deeply meditated understanding of the life of that institution's founder: 'And the Lord turned and looked upon Peter.' We are a long way from the searching reality suggested by the mention of that glance in the picture offered of Peter's handling of the affair of Ananias and Sapphira. The factuality both of the reference to Jesus' look upon Peter in the moment of the latter's betrayal and of the apparent execution of the two dishonest participants in the early church's essay on communism may well be challenged. What is significant for our purposes is the contrast in understanding realised in the two narratives. In the one we are presented with human failure, with judgement remorselessly pronounced upon that failure, but also with a compassion that is indeed the very obverse side of the coin of that condemnation. In the later tale we are presented with a picture of a struggling emergent institution already behaving to those who seem by dishonesty to threaten its policies with that ruthlessness which has across the ages characterised virtually every style of ecclesiastical institution. The survival of the institution, the effective continuance of its purpose, are presented in the tale in Acts 5 as justifying action that is none the less morally monstrous because it is presented as achieved by supernatural means. 'It is expedient that one man and one woman should die for the people.' It is only when Luke's attention is deflected from the busy life of the struggling institution that he is enabled to recall and to present with unchallengeable depth of tragic insight the bitter choices out of which indeed the institution came.

If these considerations have any validity, they suggest that whatever the Christian religion may bring to men, it does not offer them anything that can easily be represented as a 'solution of the problem of evil', or any recipes for living which will enable them to endure suffering in sure confidence that they serve an end by which their endurance will be justified or the evil which they have brought unwittingly into being by consequence of their fidelity will be somehow blotted out. The apologist, always by circumstance the servant of an institution which, however exalted in its direction, must sooner or later find in its survival and extension justification of all that is done in its name, will urge otherwise, pointing to signs that the tragic dimensions of its actual history, and of its *raison d'être* can somehow be made to disappear. If we recall here remarks made in previous sections of this book on the subject of metaphysics, we may say that we discern here the resonance within Christian theology of the age-old breach between pluralist and monist metaphysical styles. The pluralist will always insist that it is better to attempt an inventory of the different sorts of things there are in the world, and eschew any attempt at premature reduction, than seek to reveal the irreducibly diverse as in their diversity somehow expressive of a unitary whole. In the history of philosophy the pluralist has frequently laid himself open to charges of irrationality at the hands of his opponent. Further, at a relatively early stage in his philosophical career, Bertrand Russell remarked that the pluralist must necessarily in the end find himself an atheist. It would be foolish to ignore the insight of this second judgement; but one could claim that Christianity, properly understood, might provide men with a faith through which they are enabled to hold steadfastly to the significance of the tragic, and thereby protect themselves against that sort of synthesis which seeks to obliterate by the vision of an all-embracing order the sharper discontinuity of human existence. At the outset of this whole section of this book, it was of course implied that tragedy, regarded as a form of discourse, itself provided a way of representing the relation of the familiar to the transcendent. Am I now suggesting that this way of representation is somehow its own justification? Certainly this charge must be met and it can only be met if, with further examples, we turn to explore the way in which in tragedy reference to transcendence insinuates itself into what is sought. Thus, the question of the extent to which such insinuation can be regarded as valid may be opened up and its answer even slightly advanced.

12

Ethics and tragedy

We have been concerned at one and the same time with two problems; firstly, with the status of tragedy as a means of representing the relations of the familiar to the transcendent, and secondly, the claims of these representations to advance beyond other rival methods of representation in setting at rest sceptical doubts concerning all such discursive reasoning. We have to consider the suggestion that in tragedy we reach a form of representation that by the very ruthlessness of its interrogation enables us to project as does no available alternative, our ultimate questioning.

It is clear that tragedy very often finds its origin in the sort of situation that traditional moralists called 'the conflict of duties', which they sought to resolve by developing a doctrine of the moral criteria. That very phrase recalls old-fashioned debates, for instance, between teleological moralists, whether utilitarian or of more sophisticated commitment, and intuitionists. In particular one is reminded of the peculiar temper of Joseph Butler's ethics, his almost obsessive pluralism, both where the springs of human action are concerned and where the factors, with which the agent who would not defy the reality of his nature as a whole must reckon, are acknowledged. Butler's insight is shown by his hostility to any oversimplification of the human situation. If he resists Shaftesbury's attempted reduction of all human virtue to a disinterested and disciplined benevolence as neglectful of the (at least) equally stringent claims of truth and justice, he also refuses Wollaston's abstract rationalism, insisting by reference to the episode of David and Bathsheba that the sources of men's most elaborate essays in self-deception must be sought, or in some recognisably human appetite, concern, for instance, for the power that issues from a good reputation, or dread of the sorts of criticism from which men suppose that they can only protect themselves by masquerading.

Yet, in human life men must choose and their choices will reflect inevitably the sort of men they are. If they must reckon with the complexity of their human nature, they must do so in situations that are very often not of their own making. Butler's ethical doctrine is ultimately individualistic for all its author's insistence that Hobbes is radically mistaken in his psychological egoism when, for instance, he argues that sympathy is not reducible to a form of fear for oneself, activated by the sight of another's predicament. Again, Butler is wise enough to notice that men and women are frequently deflected from the path of prudence by the sort of emotional disturbance for which there is little room in the utilitarian's world. Yet he sees men's nature as something within their own power; this, though there is nothing arbitrary in the form in which a man must follow the dictates of his conscience.

At an earlier stage in this work, reference was made to the significance of the parabolic. May I refer now to another, one of the best-known of all Jesus' parables, that of the two brothers? We are presented with a piece of human life, with a triangular relation between three men, two brothers and their father. No doubt it is the function of the parable to enable men and women to glimpse in the father's ready reception of his younger son on the latter's return from the far country, the readiness of God to accept men and women in bitter need springing from their own folly and worse, with uninhibited readiness that overcomes their hesitation and removes the fears that must accompany their return. But as a piece of human life the tale is saturated with ambiguities. The father may remind us sometimes of Lear at the outset of Shakespeare's play when, in his dotage, he responds to the flattery of Goneril and Regan in self-indulgent gratification of their hopes, and rejects the sharp but devoted honesty of Cordelia. There is in the father of the parable the making of a Lear.

If it is said that such a sequel lies beyond the parable as it is recorded, one can only say that it is a tribute to the human reality of the tale that the father's weakness is not obscured by this, that his attitude towards his wayward and extravagant son is commended as an analogy of the relation of God to human beings in their frailty. In that relationship in the particular circumstances of his son's return, we are encouraged to glimpse an analogue of an ultimate mercy. Thus, the note of commendation cannot be disregarded. But the one who is thus commended remains a human being, even as his elder son remains a human being in his perfectly intelligible indignation that during the years in which he had worked at home, one may presume to maintain the value of his father's estate, he has never been encouraged to entertain his friends with the lavishness with which his father proposes to welcome his returning son. One must not forget that this son, having received his share of his father's estate, converted it into ready money and wasted it in self-indulgent living. These resources are irretrievably dissipated and if there is the wherewithal to celebrate the prodigal's return, this is due to his elder brother's very different use of his share of his inheritance and the way in which he has devoted himself to maintain the family's security. His indignation is wholly intelligible and his father's reply, while reminding him that after all he had in fact only to ask for the sort of entertainment he mentioned for it to be laid on, may strike the reader as curiously cold; 'Son, thou art always with me and all that I have is thine.' One wishes to ask the old man why then he had not made it plain, not merely in general terms, but with the sort of party the hard-working, dull, elder brother suggests now that he had always wanted, and which might in fact have made him a more forthcoming, less unattractively puritanical human being. For if the parable affirms the power of love to recreate a life, we may well ask whether that same love should not equally avail to transform the grave, disciplined prudence of the industrious.

Such commentary may seem unduly sophisticated. But what it seems to bring out is the deep, characteristic human ambiguity with which this parable is saturated, which indeed makes it significantly different from an allegory. Arguably the same might be said (and here even more I risk the charge of excess of sophistication and of needless repetition[1]) of the parable of the good Samaritan. It is manifestly concerned to throw into the clearest possible light the style of behaviour that in concrete human need is a fulfilment of the commandment that men shall love their neighbours as themselves. The Samaritan is free immediately to respond to the need of the injured man. Even as in Luke's story of the healing of the ten lepers, it is only the Samaritan who is not bound by the duty of showing himself to the priest for the proper liturgical completion of his cleansing, who is therefore free to return to thank the man who has healed him, so in the story the Samaritan has no duties such as priest and levite that must constrain them to avoid ritual impurity of contact with a possible corpse. They go on their way and no doubt in their prayers they will make mention of the victim. But the Samaritan crosses the road and binds up the wounds of the injured man, pouring in oil and wine, the former for its therapeutic and the latter for its antiseptic

[1] See chapters 7 and 8.

properties. But his action does not end there. He conveys the injured man to an inn where he will be better cared for than by the roadside, receiving something more than the first aid which his rescuer gave him. He leaves money with the innkeeper and departs, promising to pay any balance due in a subsequent visit.

What at first sight is especially commended is the uninhibited spontaneity of the Samaritan's action. But because, again, we have to reckon with a piece of life, this spontaneity is portrayed as balanced by a certain elementary skill in first aid; the mention of his use of oil and wine is extremely significant. Again he is aware of the limitations of what he can do, of the care which the man requires that in the circumstances he cannot give. So he conveys the victim to a place where he can receive more sustained and arguably more thoroughly professional care. A point of great significance is being made here. Priest and levite (as I said before) could claim that by passing by on the other side they were exercising a proper sense of discipline, refraining from any well-intentioned but possibly disastrous attempt to do for the injured man what they could not do. In the parable it is suggested that in this disciplined indifference they are without excuse. But one could claim that their action receives a partial vindication by the prudent self-discipline with which the Samaritan balances his spontaneity. He loves his neighbour as himself, not simply by allowing himself to become involved, but by ensuring that that involvement shall be to the advantage of the man he is seeking to help. It will only be to his advantage if what he himself does is wholly within the limits of his competence. Hence the conclusion of his service of the man he befriended. He loves his neighbour as himself in that by this restraint he shows that he will not convert his neighbour's need to which he has thus responded, into an opportunity for his own gratification.

'The simple art of being kind is all this poor world needs.' This doggerel is quoted if only because the phrase with which it opens expresses a pervasive moral illusion, namely the illusion that kindness is a simple matter. To deny that it is so is not to belittle simplicity. Rather it is to remind oneself of lessons taught certainly by history, recognised by moralists and regularly presented with depth of insight into the human reality beyond the competence of the average academic, in great literature. It is arguably not the Attilas who ride through blood to a throne and maintain their rule by merciless oppression, who achieve the deepest and most perilous domination over their fellows. 'What shall it profit a man if he gain the whole world and lose his soul?' The man who should strain his ears to catch that most searching question is not the man who has enlarged his resources by enterprises as savagely concluded as they were ruthlessly conceived and executed. Rather it is the man whom his fellows with good reason acclaim as their benefactor, who indeed has, almost unknown to himself, enlarged his private image both of himself and of his role by singularly generous service to others. We are familiar with the nearly ridiculous figure that, for instance, a highly successful doctor of medicine may cast, when he allows his vanity to grow under the influence of the tributes paid to his skill. The reality of the skill remains and of the good he had done by its means; but his vanity makes him almost pathetic by reason of the triviality of the little dignities he seems to regard as his due. Yet, in action that is in its fruits and indeed in its intention a genuine service of one man by another there is always the threat of a deeper corruption. Thus, the clinical psychiatrist will insist that one of the most destructive states of affairs that may develop in the course of an analysis is the analyst's working a counter-transference on to the patient whom he is treating. But in very various far less specialised situations, human beings are made desperately aware of the extent to which their response to the needs of another person may quickly assume the character of a masquerade of whose falsity they are indeed themselves particularly ignorant. The last springs to life in their soul in the context of action which to all outward seeming is quite free from self-regard, but at a deeper level is motivated by an unacknowledged egoism.

To write in these terms may seem to advance a long way beyond the human simplicities of the situation set out in the parable. Certainly the parable presented in the story of the good Samaritan is far more completely rounded than would appear at a casual reading. But it may be legitimate tribute to the narrative's reality to allow oneself to ponder the sorts of lesson that may be learnt from the Samaritan's prudent restraint. One may also set over against the parable as we have it another which brings out very sharply the case for priest and levite, a parable in which indeed the Samaritan crosses the road only to find that his hands are infected and the oil that he had used gone rancid. For human beings are not thrust into the sorts of situation to which they must respond as agents perfectly designed to suit the emergencies that they must meet. Their failure may be predictable from the very first, whether that failure takes the shape of the sort of disintegration that may quickly follow an amateurish effort to do good, or a yielding to the profound temptation born of receiving the kinds of rewards and status that will make altogether inaudible the question: What shall it profit a man?[2] In the situation to which the good Samaritan responds, after his response and the preservation of the victim's life by his effort, there is the possibility of tragedy. One could concede the situation developing in such a way that, while the victim was saved from the effect of the brutal violence of the 'muggers' who had struck him down, he was by the circumstances of his rescue placed at the mercy of his saviour. It is not simply by their flaws that men and women are betrayed, but by the activation of those flaws, in action which in itself deserves commendation.

'I am amongst you as he that doth serve.' In Luke's account of Jesus' last Passover with his disciples, he mentions a dispute among them which should be regarded as the greatest. The suggestion is clear that, as the hour of Jesus' supreme temptation draws on, so the circle of those whom he has gathered around him who have, in his own words, continued with him in his testings, begins to break up. The implication is one of a certain deliberate unwillingness even to consider the dreadful possibilities that lie immediately ahead. There is a good time coming and their master is cast for a role likely to have such tremendous importance that it is a matter of vital concern which of them shall have precedence as his vice-gerent or what you will. Jesus replies by asking them whether at a meal the diners or the servants are the superiors. The answer is obvious; it is the diners (we have to remember that it is for a meal of profound significance in the Jewish calendar that the *chaburah* of which Jesus is the centre is met together). Jesus does not dispute the obvious, only remarks that he is among them as a servant. The reader who knows also the tradition of the washing of Jesus' disciples' feet by their master on (supposedly) the same occasion, preserved by St John, is inevitably reminded of that action and even of Peter's first indignant repudiation of his master's humility.

Yet it would be a grave mistake to neglect the sombre irony whereby in fact in many human situations it is the one who serves who, by that service, makes his beneficiary his bondslave. There is an arrogance, a human pretension in the gesture of washing the travel-stained feet of one's disciples, that may be altogether absent from the

---

[2] There is also the reality of profound self-deception, issuing in the corruption of motives, and indeed in the wilful concealment by an agent from himself of what he is about.

action of a man who, with a certain degree of detached profession-
alism, fulfils highly significant tasks of government and administration. In the first years of the 'welfare state', there were those who
lamented the substitution of an impersonal administrative process
for so-called personal charity in the meeting of elementary human
needs. It was suggested that, by making poverty, illness and the like
in principle matters of administrative action, humanity was somehow banished from the relationship between those in need of relief
and those concerned to see that as far as possible the need in question was met. Yet repeatedly one was made aware that the needy
preferred the impersonality, even though, of course, inevitably
it quickly raised problems of the effective humanisation of a
bureaucratic machine, because in their new situation they were able
to claim at least a measure of what they needed as matter of right.
They were not at the receiving end of others' charity, too often
made aware that by such charity those who gave it were serving
themselves and their image of themselves at a profounder level than
that at which they helped those to whom they claimed to be bringing relief. One can go further and say that if the average man were
to attempt something as extravagant as the washing of his fellows'
feet, he would be indulging in a melodramatic gesture. It is the sort
of action that might have entered the fantasies of Joseph Conrad's
Lord Jim, the kind of imagined service of his fellows which in antici-
pation he saw himself performing that, by the manner in which he
conceived it, helped to make inevitable his failure in the concrete
emergency in which on his ship he had to act. Further, in Conrad's
remarkable exploration, Jim is presented as so bemused by his own
sense of what one day he will do that he cannot accept his jumping
from his ship in the moment of supreme emergency for what it
actually was.[3] If Jesus is able to say that he is among his friends as
their servant, and conveys the reality of that status by his action,
it is only out of his total interior self-consecration to his Father's will
that he is enabled so to speak to act without taint of ambiguity. It is
only because his face has been steadfastly set to go to Jerusalem that
his ready fraternising with the disreputable is innocent of all suggestion of emotional self-indulgence. But, though his service of his
fellows which reaches its term in his laying down of his life, is in
this respect free of ambiguity, yet as we have seen, in many other
respects it remains profoundly tragic.

[3] I owe much to Dr Tony Tanner's valuable monograph on this novel, *Studies
in English Literature*, No. 12 (Edward Arnold, 1963).

So the parables' counsel by their suggestion of the ways of God with men, of the style of the good neighbour, is pregnant at once with the profoundest illumination and also with a built-in peril of misapprehension. And the same is true of Jesus' actions. For if at one level they are indeed the paradigm reality to which the parables point, the reception of the guilty that is altogether without illusion, the offer of a consolation that is without threat of corrupting self-enhancement through the giving, yet as we have seen, the tragic is not eluded; rather, in the moment of victory, the conqueror's achievement is almost overshadowed by terrible and in part foreseeable consequences. To receive Christ's service of his fellows for what it was may be accounted a task far beyond the majority of men.

At the beginning of this chapter mention was made of the old-fashioned problem of the conflict of duties or claims (to use the term employed in discussing this conflict by the late Professor H. A. Prichard) in human situations. Men and women are often confronted with conflicting claims, unable to fulfil both of them, unable also to reconcile the conflict by defining that which they ought to do more inclusively. The claims which thus conflict go far beyond the range of examples often mentioned in traditional treatises of moral philosophy – this partly because the claims upon the individual in a given situation must include his duty towards himself. One of the factors with which he must reckon is the stuff of which he is made, the built-in inheritance of his early years and environment, the flaws developed in his character while he was still at the mercy of those charged with his nurture. A measure of self-knowledge is quite properly regarded as a constituent of any human maturity; but such self-knowledge may inhibit action, may face a man with a choice of turning aside from a task which circumstance has thrust upon him or in risk of the consequences respond to its demand. In his remarkable study of Sophocles' Oedipus the King[4] Mr Phillip Vellacott, emphasising the obvious preoccupation of the dramatist with the theme of self-knowledge (treated in a very different way by Socrates and Plato), suggests that Oedipus half-knew what he was doing in his marriage to Jocasta. Such an interpretation links Sophocles' drama with the Socratic preoccupation with self-knowledge, and also with Plato's continued preoccupation with the question of the relation of knowledge and opinion, suggesting in many places that the latter represents a kind of half-knowledge, occupying a sort of no-man's-land between the kind of reasoned insight which a man

[4] Sophocles and Oedipus (Macmillan, 1971).

may properly call knowledge and the state of ignorance. Mr Vellacott suggests for instance that we can hardly suppose that a man as intelligent as Oedipus arriving in Thebes inevitably disturbed, by news of its king's violent death on the road, should not have linked the circumstances of that death with the ending of the brawl in which he had himself been involved with an irascible elderly traveller not many days before. Yet when, by exercise of that same intelligence Oedipus has freed the city from the menace of the Sphinx, he does not hesitate to marry Jocasta and to assume the throne – this though to any man who had indeed left the home of his supposed parents in respect for the oracle that prophesied he would slay his father and marry his mother, there was something risky in taking for a wife a woman old enough to have borne him. If Vellacott is right, Oedipus' guilt is that of a kind of overboldness, and this he claims we discern in the uneven but strenuously maintained manner in which he conducts the enquiry into the cause of the plague that has smitten Thebes, more than half suspecting that in the end that enquiry will focus on himself. One recalls his departure from Corinth and acknowledges that he took the road which in the end led him to Thebes and to the disaster that preceded and followed his arrival, out of respect for the oracle and out of devotion to his foster-parents. In a sense he is betrayed into guilt by an effort initiated in order to avoid it. But if Mr Vellacott is right, at a certain moment his will to maintain his innocence and to preserve others from involvement in his fate is undermined. Yet how is it undermined? In part by his coming to a city whose life is dominated by a ghastly inhuman menace, and using his remarkable endowment of intelligence to banish the monster forever, when he answers the riddle of the Sphinx and the monster throws herself from the cliff.

It may be over-sophisticated to ask the question whether Oedipus should have involved himself in the Thebes situation. One must remember of course that before he did so, according to the legend, he had already slain his father. But he had not yet committed incest nor begotten the four children whose sombre history has already been recalled. One can say of course that he was the victim of a destiny he could not escape. But this destiny fastens its grasp upon him through the invitation to come to the help of those in strange and bitter need. Again, we notice ambiguity. First there is the ambiguity of Oedipus' betrayal into guilt in consequence of the effort to avoid it by flight from Corinth. Then, secondly, there is the confusion in which, if Mr Vellacott is right, he wills to live, that besets his early years in Thebes. In Sophocles' version of the play he brings disaster in the first instance in the form of the plague; but it is through his service that the disaster comes upon the city.

We can think of comparable cases of conflict of claims far less remote from us than this most famous and most powerfully presented myth, conflict of claims in which one of the claims that we must weigh is that of the stringency of the course of action which self-knowledge counsels. It may be that we are not of the stuff of which those who would right wrongs, bring comfort to the suffering, see through to the end a complex task of government and administration, are made. In Shakespeare's play Hamlet bitterly railed against the circumstance that cast him for the role to set the affairs of Denmark aright. 'The times are out of joint.' It is upon him that the duty has devolved by bitter retribution upon his father's murderers to excise the rottenness that has infected his kingdom. He is called to a work of retributive justice, that within the framework of the play can only be accomplished by a personally executed revenge; he has himself to slay his stepfather. The work is quite simply too much for him, and as every reader of the play knows, the attempt to carry it out brings into the open the deep ambiguity of his relationship with his mother and leads him to destroy Ophelia. To attempt to summarise in a few sentences the profundity of Shakespeare's exploration of the human psyche in this play would be ridiculous. But for my purposes it is enough to say that here again we face the tragic reality of the conflict of duties in a situation in which a man, in order to serve what he supposes to be the cause of truth and justice, must out of his weakness destroy himself and in destroying himself bring equally irretrievable disaster upon those, such as Ophelia, he is involved with.

It is when one allows one's attention to fasten upon the sorts of exploration of the human reality that we have here reviewed that we come to recognise the paradox that, while in one way a proper respect for the irreducibility of the tragic inhibits ambitious metaphysical construction, in another the sort of commentary on human life which one finds in the tragedies here reviewed and the parables analysed, makes one in the end discontented with any sort of naturalism. It is as if we are constrained in pondering the extremities of human life to acknowledge the transcendent as the only alternative to the kind of trivialisation which would empty of significance the sorts of experience with which we have been concerned.

13

The notion of presence

The distinction drawn by Professor Strawson between descriptive and revisionary metaphysics is one of very great importance. But it would be a mistake to identify this distinction with the distinction which Kant draws between the sort of metaphysics which he allows and the transcendent metaphysics which he insists, by argument (sometimes as tortuous as it is strenuous) to be invalid. If Kant has anything in the nature of a revisionary metaphysics it is to be identified with his system as a whole, with the revaluation of human experience that it effects. It is indeed with this revaluation that we have been concerned in the sections of this work devoted to discussion of the so-called primacy of the practical reason. It was Kant's achievement to suggest that only a most thoroughgoing metaphysical agnosticism could establish this primacy as invulnerable. One of the questions which the study of his philosophy leaves unanswered is the question of the ultimate tenability of this point of view. Indeed, part of the purpose of this work has been to examine the extent to which the problem of transcendent metaphysics remains, indeed, receives after Kant's work a sharp articulation.

   The most elementary student of Kant's philosophy quickly learns the extent to which alongside his rigorously professional critique of the claims of the transcendent metaphysician there runs a parallel impulse. He would suggest almost that we know all along that the man is wasting his time, that these problems are sorted and settled in the way we want them settled. This we shall see if only we can make ourselves realise that the impulse to take them seriously comes from practical concerns and is not the expression of a detached intellectual curiosity. Indeed, we know this as soon as we ponder the significance of our readiness to reject materialism and to accept the equally untenable alternative view of the world's origin and nature, as we have already proved on our pulses the latter to be true and the former false. The language used here is of course not worthy of the very great philosopher whose work we are reviewing. It has a starkness, even a vulgarity that his German philosophical prose avoids, whatever the other faults of which it may be justly accused. To speak in this way is to suggest that Kant supposes men's allegiance always to be enlisted on the side of the angels, only too quick to use their intellectual dexterity to conceal from themselves a commitment in which their nature necessarily involves them. Metaphysical argument, even indulgence in the wrong sort of agnostic appraisal of its inconclusive outcome, may be a way of deceiving ourselves concerning what is present to us all the time. To suggest that we must wait before engaging with a temptation – to practise self-deceit on the refutation of the moralist's argument, is to seek to dodge the issue, pleading that facing it must wait the unattainable. A proper agnosticism will set us free from such hesitation and thrust us back on the road that we must follow anyhow.

Yet the reader will notice that in this summary exposition of Kant's views, I have made use of the notion of presence, and this notion, as we shall see in the section that immediately follows, is one deeply fraught with ontological undertones and overtones. If we say that in moral experience transcendence is present to us all along, how are we using the language that we employ? What sort of presence is this of which we speak? The problem is of course at least as old as Plato's highly sophisticated discussion of the notion of *parousia* in the first half of the *Parmenides*. It is to critical analysis of this notion that I wish to turn, asking the reader to bear with a very unsophisticated introduction.

When one speaks of presence, arguably one thinks first of presence in space. Thus, when we say that we have been admitted to someone's presence, we are likely to be referring first to the fact that spatial barriers between us have been removed. The door is open and we see the great man in front of us. So too we speak of the presence in a room of articles of furniture; or we say that we are vaguely aware of a presence in a place we had good reason to suppose unoccupied. Here the implication of our words would normally involve reference to a living thing, even to a source of menace to our safety. More loosely, we speak of friends whose presence we miss, either because they are now elsewhere or because they are dead. If we say that we miss their presence because they are dead, we are of course altering the force of the word. Absence is one thing, death is another. If we say that death has removed someone from our presence, we seem to suggest an analogy with the absence of someone who has gone on a long journey. But death is not a journey; if we speak of it as such, immediately we must remind ourselves that it takes men to that bourne from which 'no traveller returns', and again this failure to return is no matter of permanent settlement in a realm remote from us which we know that we shall not visit. We speak of a final, an ultimate, absence, and in doing so we refer obliquely to what is irreducibly unique by reference to one of its effects.

Of course sometimes when we speak of 'presence', we speak of what is contemporary; the emphasis here is temporal, not spatial. Thus, a philosopher may say that his present views of a particular problem differ markedly from those set out in an article published a few years previously. Here, the immediate force of the word *presence* is emphasis on the simultaneity of the opinions he holds and his words about them. What he says is what he thinks at the time he speaks. This then undoubtedly possesses a spatially measurable physiological correlate; but in this place it is legitimate to avoid begging any questions concerning the reducibility of thought to terms of such an alleged correlate. If thinking involves an element irreducibly mental, that element is presumably in time but not necessarily in space. It may indeed be true that as a matter of psychological fact, we spatialise time in order to think it. If I see my views on the approaching Czechoslovak–German crisis in the summer of 1938 as relatively naive and uninformed as they developed in the hot months of that unforgettable summer, I am referring to private musings, arguments within myself as well as with friends; I am referring to what certainly occupied periods of time, sometimes still vividly recalled, even when the recollection is shot through with shame at my naivety. But inevitably, as I think these past, largely private experiences, the images whereby I focus attention on what I recall are spatial. In recollection of one's most private experience, that may have had existence only as a modification of oneself, inevitably one represents the event by a spatial image. The relation of present to past evokes immediate spatialisation; this, though one is aware that what one thus spatialises *may* be gravely misrepresented by such an image. Still more, of course, when one comes to events relative to one another in a public time and one requires surrogates to represent this time or chronometers to measure it, one finds the former in selected spatial symbols, the latter, it may be, in selected cyclical processes, whose uniformity is stable and unaffected relatively by environmental change.

These reflections deliberately seem random; they are concerned to introduce the formal complexity of the notion of presence in ordinary everyday usage. A scholar may rejoice to have his books beside him again and may express his happiness by the somewhat exalted idiom of speaking of himself as again in the presence of his friends. A woman may lament the disappearance of her pet cat; she does not need the language of presence to express her joy when the animal reappears, dusty, a little tired, and keeping its own counsel where it has been during its disturbing absence from home. The cat is back, sleeping again in its basket. It may be indeed that there is very often in ordinary usage something a little exalted intended by choice of the word presence. Thus, a hero-worshipper may speak of his emotions at finding himself in the presence of his hero. Again, the student of mass political psychology in the twentieth century is aware of the charismatic power exerted by certain political leaders in the first instance on those whom they are immediately addressing face to face, but also at a remove from those who hear their voice over the radio. Thus, to refer again in this connection to the events of 1938, no one who heard Hitler's speech in the Sports Palace in Berlin on the night of Monday 26 September of that year, will ever forget the note of madness that sounded unmistakably in his screaming, nor the clear evidence of the infectious power of this insanity afforded by the cries of his followers as they responded to him. No doubt there were many listening over the radio who were moved to share the savage emotion his words aroused on that occasion in those who both saw and heard him. To his followers in the stadium he was visibly present; to those who heard him he was also present audibly and many of those hearers certainly made their own responses with those gathered round him. Others heard and were horrified. Immediately, one asks questions concerning the difference in his presence to them and his presence to his devotees. Both alike reacted, the devotees by a fiercely answering *Sieg Heil*, the others, it may be, by an equally emphatic but differently phrased No, or even by a prayer for deliverance. In the last case he certainly had on them the effect a man may only have when (to use a familiar idiom), he 'makes his presence felt'. And here one speaks of his presence in the world, including the effect he has on those immediately exposed to his influence. So the musing continues; there is something specialised in the idiom of presence. One speaks more readily of coming and going, of departure and return, even of a sudden return of one long absent, eagerly awaited, whose train is suddenly at the platform (or so it seems, almost as if the last hours of the long period of separation are cut short and the appearance again of the one long missed assumes a kind of unexpected quality). If one continues these reflections, one is made aware quite quickly of the extent to which presence and absence are elements of limitation in characteristically human experience. If I am in one place, I am not in another. If I am at present appreciating the quiet of the room in which I am writing, I am, by the fact that I am in that room and not elsewhere, debarred from all sorts of experience that I might even now be enjoying if I were not where I am, engaged on this task and not another.

Again, my life has been lived during the period that separates the present from my birth. There is a sense in which I must regard what happened before I was born as unknown to me. To say that is not to forget that the period is well enough documented for it to be rubbish for me to pretend that I do not know a very great deal about it. But there is a perfectly intelligible sense in which I can say that I do not know what it was like to live in the reign of Edward VII in the way in which my parents did. It is a commonplace of course to say that in a perfectly good sense I may know a great deal more about that period than they did. Yet they lived through it and I did not. The experience of living through it was part of their lives; it never will be part of mine. If a man enlarges his experience, he is only able to do so by what is accessible to him. Clearly, the limits of accessibility are greatly widened in the case of a man whose historical imagination is at once disciplined and informed, wide-ranging and sympathetic. Yet, the barriers remain. Thus, a very distinguished historian of the Tudor period spoke of his emotion on listening to madrigals which once those men and women heard, on whom for many years his historical study had been concentrated. He heard what they heard and sometimes (if I recall his words aright) he felt that his response was akin to theirs; but then this hope would vanish and he would wonder whether he had not to say that the music to which he responded was by that very response rendered irreducibly different from what the men and women of the late sixteenth century had heard with joy. The traditional theological doctrine of divine omnipresence presumably before all else was concerned to insist that where God is concerned these limitations do not apply. If a child prays to God as everywhere present, he means that someone the child loves from whom he is separated is in no sense separated from God. Where he is concerned (if he exists) distinctions between here and there and indeed between past and present and future, do not apply, if indeed they apply at all, as they do in human experience. To pretend that they do is inevitably to lapse into anthropomorphism, and this danger certainly besets the unsophisticated religious imagination which would content itself with the affirmation that God is everywhere present. For what is this presence that is without absence? Can we concede it? But in these deep metaphysical waters we need not at this moment attempt to keep afloat, as our purpose is much more circumscribed.

We are in fact concerned with the way in which we can significantly speak of the transcendent as impinging upon our experience, as being present in stretches of that experience. In 1950 Mr R. H. S. Crossman edited a volume entitled *The God that Failed*, which included statements by a number of persons who had been card-carrying members of the Communist Party during the Stalinist period, who for one reason or another had abandoned their Communist faith. In many ways the most interesting of these statements was the first, by Arthur Koestler, which included material not to be found either in his famous novel *Darkness at Noon* (1941) or in his autobiographical essay *Spanish Testament* (1937). It is to this material that we turn in order to develop, by reference to one undoubtedly interesting example, the question which I have in mind.

In 1936 Koestler was covering the Spanish Civil War for the (now defunct) *News Chronicle*. He was taken prisoner by Franco's forces and was found by his captors to be a card-carrying member of the Communist Party. At that time, anyone taken prisoner by the rebels against the Spanish Republican Government who was found in possession of such a card was sentenced to death. In the jail in which Koestler found himself, awaiting execution, he heard every morning towards first light the agents of the 'White Terror' going about their grisly work of execution. Thus, he heard the noise of doors opening and shutting, the cries, the screams, the whimpers, the terrible rattle of gunfire as the firing squad eliminated in the name of Franco's new order those they judged unfit to live in the Spain they hoped to build. As he listened Koestler recalls in his essay that he became gradually aware that what was being done was destructive of what he described as the very human law of gravity, the analogue in the human world to the sort of universal operative force that Newton formulated in the dynamical equations of his inverse square law. The kind of mental respect that must govern human beings in their relation to each other was imperilled by the kind of petty indifference to weakness that he experienced in the behaviour of his captors towards those whom they had at their mercy. But he did not stop there; rather he began to realise that as a Stalinist, he was himself guilty of a comparable contempt for the human. The time of his imprisonment (1936–7) was the period which saw the unfolding of the 'great purge'; the terrible events that followed Stalin's decision to adopt the policies of radical industrialisation favoured by his great antagonist, Trotsky, lay already several years in the past. A kind of moral corruption to which Stalinism committed the Party member was already too evident for Koestler to pretend for one moment that he was not, as long as he remained a Communist, guilty. He uses an extraordinarily telling image in order to force on himself the character of the moral evil of which he judges both his captors and himself to be guilty. If the philosophically sophisticated reader is reminded of Kant in the way in which Koestler insists on the universal authority of a principle, he is also reminded of that remarkable passage in Kant's *Tugendlehre* in which, in a slightly different but still related connection, the German moralist uses the same image as Koestler employs.[1] In the passage in the *Tugendlehre* (to summarise its argument again) in which Kant talks of love, he insists that when two human beings love each other there must obtain in their relationship something analogous to gravitation, the complementary operation of attractive and repulsive force. One human being may be drawn to another (and Kant is clearly thinking both of sexual love and of friendship); there is an obvious attraction between them. Indeed, in speaking of them of being drawn to one another, one is already using this idiom. But out of this attraction may come two consequences, both alike damaging. One person may seek to dominate the other, to impose upon the other his views of the world, indeed of their relationship. Alternatively, one person may become infatuated with the one he believes himself to love so that the other (it may be unintentionally) becomes the occasion of a sort of infatuation as destructive of authentic relationship as the kind of egoistic domination mentioned a moment ago. In both cases the outcome is destructive. It is Kant's view that such domination can only be avoided when a proper respect enables each of the two to hold the other at a certain distance, seeking neither to dominate nor to yield to a sort of slavish subordination. Here there is in Kant's view a complementarity analogous to that supplied in gravity by the repulsion which balances attraction.

The image (as I suggested in chapter 5 of this work) is as powerful in Kant as it is in Koestler. It certainly enables the reader to lay hold for himself upon the point which Kant is making. There is of course

[1] Reference has been made to this passage in chapter 5.

no suggestion at all of any kind of ontological analogy of being between gravity and human relationships. It is simply a case of a very
powerful image being used to give the reader an unshakeable grip on
a very significant moral reality. Koestler's situation is different and
the kind of lesson he sought to teach himself by the use of the same
image, related but distinguishable. Yet in his case also it is through
the image that the lesson is learned.

I am not wishing for one moment to suggest any sort of ontological
continuity between the abstract physical reality captured in Newton's equation and the human reality that concerns the moralist or
the prisoner. Rather, to revert to Koestler's situation, it is in its
situation that the moral reality is disclosed as present and disclosed
to him for what it is when he uses a powerful image in order to lay
hold of it. *The use of the image is indeed part of the experience,* and
therefore in so far as it is in the experience that the reality is said
to be present, we can say certainly that it is through the image that
that presence is realised and rendered effective.

Thus, we return again to one of the central themes of this study,
that was raised in the earlier discussion of the relation between
realism and constructivism. We have here an experience of quite
peculiar intensity; indeed it is the experience of a man who had good
reason to believe that he was shortly to die in the same way as those
whose terrible ends he overheard. Yet, by this situation, his perception is intensified and he is aware of violations of the human substance to which he has been privy and which he must now repudiate.
The repudiation is imposed upon him as an imperative and it is
only through accepting its imperative force that he learns the lesson
his situation may teach him. But he makes this imperative force plain
to him by the image that he employs. It is not that the imperative
ceases to be an imperative; rather the image enables him to represent
to himself the pattern of human life which his complicity in Stalin's
tyranny commits him to violate. He sees this pattern as something
woven into the scheme of things. It is not that he is commanded by
strenuous effort of will to affirm a particular view of the world.
Rather he is called to sustain something from which he knows he
derives his own moral substance; a threat to it is in the end a menace
to himself. He needs an idiom in which the formal distinction
between 'ought' and 'is' is broken down and he finds it in the powerfully suggestive image of the law of gravity. It is a commonplace of
course to insist that laws of nature are not laws that a man may
break in the way in which he breaks the criminal law of the state in

which he lives. One is often reminded that if a man thinks to defy the law of gravity in walking over the edge of a cliff, he merely continues to illustrate it. Moral laws, on the other hand, are often disregarded; but there is something strange in their disregard in that if it is fundamental (as in the case of radical self-deception) it is a self-destruction. Our being is at stake here and we are compelled by what we are. Hence the powerful image of the natural law is invoked to capture the extent to which in the particular situation of a frightened prisoner there is present what is universal and what is absolute.

But of what sort of presence do we speak? Or are we simply using the word 'presence' because of all the words that occur to us it is the least misleading because the most akin to a variable to which we can give what values seem best to us? Koestler is in his prison in Malaga until such time as by the intervention of Sir Peter Chalmers-Mitchell he is delivered. In what sense, if any, may we say that what is absolute is present in his experience? We want to speak of a nearness, of an involvement; but it is not a spatial inclusion. Yet his experience takes place in the prison and it is necessary that it should for the experience to be what it is. Again, this experience followed years of complicity in Stalin's crimes and it is divisible into parts, some of which are simultaneous, one with another, as when we say, referring to an intellectual experience, that its distinguishable moments tumbled one over the other as if our mind was invaded by the overlapping constituents of a complex idea. If we speak of the presence of the absolute it is because we have no other language. Yet, by doing so in ways as tentative as those followed here, we have already moved beyond Kant. We have indeed suggested that there is a kind of ontological intrusion that makes such experience not simply a matter of wilful fantasy or even imaginative indulgence, but rather a response to what is there. But how is it there? Have we gone any way to answering that question by the intense scrutiny to which we have submitted the experience in question? But note the phrase – how is it there? The words are all monosyllables and they are all familiar. We ask of something which in fact the cat has brought in how it comes that this strange, malodorous object is where it is; later the creature's behaviour gives us all the answer we require. But what is there in Koestler's experience brought to full focus of effective presence by his idiom? There too our language is metaphorical, reminding us what has been said of Hitler's effect upon his audience.

Although I only mention the fact now, it is reflection prompted by Plato's discussion in the *Parmenides* of the relation of particulars to forms that has helped to give shape and direction to this argument. The term *presence*, on which we have chiefly concentrated, is one which he himself employs; indeed, it might be regarded as the generic term of which *participation* and *copying* are specifications. Alternatively it can be regarded as a variable to which the two latter terms attempt to assign determinate values. Plato is quite confident in rejecting the suggestion that there are forms of mud, hair and dirt, although if he were to press the argument for the reality of forms that seeks one over against the many, he would be hard put to find grounds for denying that there are forms at least of muddiness, hairiness and dirtiness. But his forms are paradigms and to treat them as if they were simply *universalia ante res* is grossly to misunderstand their import for Plato. When he goes on to speak of the senses in which particulars may be regarded as sharing in forms or as copying them in such a way as to resemble them, his whole argument achieves very little more than an effective dismissal of the suggestion that the participation and the copying involved can be regarded as co-ordinate species with sorts of sharing and of representation familiar to us in the world of everyday. If a meal is shared between a group of diners, it is eventually exhausted; if a sum of money is distributed among a number of recipients, in due course it is all used up. Again, both those who eat and the meal which they share, those who receive money and the gold that is given them, all alike belong to the same world of space and time. Certainly those who eat and those who receive the money are living human beings, while food and gold are (in different senses) inanimate objects (I say in different senses, for the food may have included flesh meat). But the food on a diner's plate is of the same sort as the food on the dish from which his fellows and himself help themselves. The gold or silver he spends in the shops is of the same sort as the gold or silver from which his share has come. Plato is fully aware that we are using relations between what is familiar to us in the world in which we live to convey the relation of that world as a whole to its transcendent ground.

Certainly, nothing can be called a copy or representation of anything else unless that something else exists to be copied. Whether one thinks of a great portrait, a passport photograph or an identikit picture, they are all alike derivative in that they are in different ways pictures of an individual human being who has his own existence apart from the representation. One could go further and say that that existence is relatively unaffected by its representation on canvas or by photograph; this, provided of course one remembers that men have been moved to anger by the artist's skill and insight displayed in their portrait. Again, if men are to be said to share a meal, that meal must first be there for them to partake of it. Again, a meal may go uneaten and those who were to have eaten it, distracted maybe by the sudden emergence into the open of suppressed emotional conflict between them, depart leaving it untasted on the table. This laboured discussion is only concerned to bring out the element of derivation between copy and original, the element of independence in what men may be said to share *vis-à-vis* their sharing it. It is well known that Plato probes deeply the contradictions quickly revealed in the attempt to work out the consequences of conceiving the relation between particular and form as resemblance. If we say that three particulars (say three men) are rightly grouped together as men in virtue of resemblance one to another and of resemblance of all three alike to a paradigm *manhood*, which all three alike imperfectly embody, do we suppose that the four (the three men and their manhood) are regarded as all four resembling one another as the three are recognised to do? If we do, are we not bound to posit a *further manhood* as that embodied in all four and warranting us to group them together as it is said we should do?[2] Plato uses such an argument particularly to bring out the paradigmatic character of the forms; they are self-existent standards and therefore they cannot properly be grouped with those who are ranged in order of achievement in their concrete particular existence, of that form which they more or less imperfectly exemplify. Thus in Books VIII and IX of the *Republic*, which contain some of the most suggestive ethical and political teaching of that very controversial work, Plato sets out a series of polities and of individual ways of life that constitute a progressive departure from the norms of justice. Thus, timocratic man, for whom courage is the highest of the virtues and whose way of life is seen in large scale in societies whose ethos is determined by a military caste, is nearer the norm than the so-called oligarch who succeeds him. But the latter is a disciplined, hard-working individual, ready to live laborious days and to postpone any form of self-indulgence to the achievement of commercial success. His virtues are those of the entrepreneur and the society whose style reflects the temper of his life, is one in which (to use modern language) economic growth is secured

---

[2] This because *manhood* is thought to resemble the three men as each resembles one another.

at the price of commonly accepted disciplines, enabling individuals to forgo every form of luxury, even quick returns, in the interest of steady increase in wealth. Yet, the oligarch is a man who has declined even from the standard professed and achieved by the timocrat. He lacks the latter's sense of honour; his life has little room for the extremities of self-disregard that men may display on the field of battle. One is reminded of the fact that where the utilitarian is concerned it is often remarked that for him prudence is the supreme human virtue. Again, one recalls the wry comment passed by Bertrand Russell on the 'philosophical radicals' who pressed the utilitarian doctrine to its furthest limits, that few men wrote more of the significance of pleasure in the ordering of human affairs, who showed themselves so little capable of simple enjoyment in their personal lives. The Puritan quality of the oligarch's self-discipline is undeniable; but it is a Puritanism practised in the name of a personal success, definable in measurable terms. But as the 'ideal declension' proceeds, the oligarch is replaced by the democrat, for Plato the man who is prepared to try everything once, who is portrayed as one who rejects every sort of discipline and every sort of principle by which one form of satisfaction is judged preferable to another. The position in which Plato deploys his criticism of democratic society and of democratic man is notorious; but provided the reader remembers that in this whole stretch of his argument Plato is giving his own sense to political and social terms which he uses, one can find in his treatment of the democratic man a savage and illuminating caricature that is drawn with a certain hardly mistakable affection for the original. But the flamboyant, experimental style that marks the democrat is replaced in due course by tyranny, and the tyrant is presented as the term of human decline from the proper norm of human life and those forms of society which are called tyranny are presented as conveying on a larger canvas the sheerly self-destructive character of the tyrant's life.

In reading the critical discussion in the *Parmenides*, it is worth while carrying this extended example in mind if only to see that the resemblance between particular and form is that between imperfect embodiment and ideal. The five ways of life that Plato is comparing in his presentation of the decline from just society to tyranny, are all alike ways of human life. But it is surely his view that the way of life of the just man (however much we may reject his view of what that way of life is) is more properly human than that of timocrat, democrat, oligarch and tyrant. If we would know what it is to live as a human being, we must look at the just man and then go on (if we are examining our own life-styles) to determine how much there is in us, for instance of oligarch, of democrat, even of half-acknowledged longing to live as we suppose the tyrants are by their power enabled to do. Compare again the use of the myth of Gyges in Book II.

We may indeed say that ways of life here compared are regarded as ways of human life by reference to the alleged norm from which progressively they diverge. We can even (drawing on the insights won by Aristotle through his criticisms of Plato) speak of another example here of relativity to 'focal meaning'. Yet two questions immediately arise. Do we suppose that the norm of the just life has been realised, that the paradigm is in some sense at our disposal? It is Plato's claim that in the whole work that precedes the section we have been considering, that is, from the beginning of Book II onwards, he has deployed both the just way of life and the means of its secure embodiment alike in individual and in institutional terms. But what he has offered (and I deliberately avert here from any sort of detailed criticism) is the diagrammatic scheme of a polity which is in itself particular, and which if it were ever realised would belong together with such other particularities of human history as the development and maintenance of the Spartan constitution, the emergence of the Athenian empire, etc. What belongs to history is particular and is of the world of space and time, of the world of coming-to-be and growth and nurture. We are not here confronted with what is transcendent. In an excellent article on the section of the *Parmenides* with which we have been concerned, Professor Peter Geach compares particular ideas or forms with the standard metre.[3] One cannot measure the standard metre; this, because it is the standard of measurement. So one cannot speak of forms as resemblants; for it is by reference to them that we decide whether or not and to what extent entities superficially as different as timocracy from tyranny in Plato's view do in fact resemble one another. Yet, if we say that we can't measure the standard metre, the ground of that impossibility is conventional and the convention would disappear if some other standard than the length of platinum in Paris were chosen as standard. True, the length of platinum is selected for this role because of its exceptional durability and indestructibility; but the length belongs to time and space as much as the building in which it

[3] Available in R. E. Allen, *Essays on Plato's Metaphysics* (Routledge and Kegan Paul, 1965).

is housed, and though it is resistant to destruction in ways in which the building is not, yet still it may be dissolved. Certainly its dissolution would unsettle the whole business of measurement of spatial magnitudes. But although measurement has its principles and foundations (as indeed Plato knew) it is still a matter of human contrivance and the destruction of the conditions of its conduct, would only occasion the need to perfect alternative devices.

There is a genuine analogy between the role of the standard metre and the role of the just man and the just city in Plato's ethics. Both alike are paradigms, but where the just man and the just city are concerned, we have to reckon with the concretion in space and time of the form of justice. This form is for Plato absolutely indestructible, and this because as it never in any sense came into being and is subject to no process of growth or of decline, it is absolutely and not relatively immune from diminution, decay, annihilation. The just city may indeed vanish from the face of the earth; but the conditions of its realisation remain in as much as those conditions include as their unconditional necessary foundation, a vision of that which is absolutely self-existent. Indeed, where the just city is concerned we have to reckon with a human polity whose significance resides in the extent to which it mediates effectively the form of the just.

Yet, if we remember that forms are paradigms (the just city only derivatively paradigmatic), we may begin to see that one of the important points that Plato is making in his argument in the *Parmenides* is the deep fallacy of allowing ourselves to treat forms as particularly privileged particulars, and thus divesting them of their peculiar authority. But when we have recognised their paradigmatic status, we have still to face up to the fact that paradigms are also part of the furniture of the world we live in. We may say that we select the just man as our paradigm of human life and seek to bring home to ourselves the implications of our choice by patient deployment of the way of life we seek to extol. We may indeed insist that the inventive imaginative genius that Plato on occasion (and not least in the books of the *Republic* with which we have been concerned here) displays in this deployment is exercised in discovery rather than romantically self-indulgent fantasy. But if we do, we have of course to defend our claim that here we discover rather than invent, or that if we invent, our invention is a way of finding rather than of fashioning. Such a defence will inevitably involve us again in the central problems of this chapter, which are indeed very near the problems with which Plato engaged in the vastly illuminating first stretch

159

of the *Parmenides*. It is as if we know where we want to arrive, yet find ourselves defeated in every attempt we make to articulate in intelligible conceptual shape the object of our exercise. We are concerned with incommensurables, with the relation of that we know not what it is to the familiar, which none the less seems to disclose itself to us in ways that we can make our own.

Koestler's experience in the Malaga jail in which he awaited execution was to him an intimation of the absolute. We cannot separate what was thus intimated from the way in which he laid hold upon it. One might say that if (as we have previously suggested) the theory of forms in the *Republic* and the dialogues belonging to the same period represents an extended, confused, vulnerable, even perverted formulation of a central metaphysical insight, that deserves to be taken seriously, partly for its very tentativeness, Koestler's fragmentary intuition when by formulation he had made it his own left him with a sounder sense of the way in which human beings should behave one towards another. Indeed, one might argue that in some respects he was more surely Socrates' disciple than Plato's, who, while he formulated with unexampled insight the metaphysical problem that Socrates' life had raised yet, in the practical policies he suggested to enable his master's insight to achieve triumphant institutional embodiment, betrayed the quizzical, interrogative spirit of the man who had inspired him.

The argument of this chapter is a unity in as much as it is concentrated upon the notion of presence and therefore inevitably turned to the writing of that metaphysician who first scrutinised the role of this concept in metaphysics, and this with special reference to his own doctrine, to his own transcendent ontology. Very early in the *Parmenides*, Plato rejects out of hand the suggestion that the forms may be regarded as *noēmata*; it is such passages that have helped to earn for the critics of constructivism in modern philosophy of mathematics, the name of Platonists. But in rejecting the suggestion that his forms are *noēmata*, Plato is implicitly rejecting any treatment of his doctrine as a way of looking at the world. In contemporary philosophy of religion it is fashionable to speak, for instance, of faith in its cognitive aspect as a 'seeing as'. Thus, it is suggested that the man of faith is enabled by the credenda he has accepted in self-commitment to Christ to see the world differently, even to find in the world thus differently seen, confirmation of its commitment. Thus, faith is identified with a commitment enabling men to see the world differently that is itself somehow confirmed by the difference in picture won through the commitment. The element of circularity is inescapable. Yet in order to be fair to this fashionable and influential point of view which is defended by many able men, may I take this example? The artist, Paul Nash, painted during the war a very remarkable landscape entitled *Totes Meer* (which hangs in the Tate Gallery); in it the painter realised as a vast Sargasso sea a great dump in which the wreckage of combat aircraft, both British and German, had been deposited. In the painting, the pictures formed by the wings and fuselage are at once wild, dead, somehow obscene. It so happened that after I had seen several reproductions of this painting (though not then the original) I passed the dump between East Oxford and Garsington which had provided the artist with the subject-matter of his composition. I knew that it was there that Nash had found his subject, when I myself passed the place, and I recall vividly that my perceptual experience was deeply affected, indeed suffused, by memory of the painting I had seen reproduced. I might say that 'I saw' the dump as 'the dead sea' which Nash had suggested with tremendous force it might be viewed as being. There is no doubt whatsoever that my perception was heightened when I first saw the dump through my knowledge of the painting; I might say that I saw more, and in the seeing was made vividly aware of the sheer waste of what, conveyed by the works of human ingenuity displayed before me, was wrecked and destroyed even as no doubt most of those who had flown them had either died or suffered injury of body and spirit. Nash had conveyed the dump as a dead sea, as an element doubly alien to men, alien not simply as the sea is alien but also alien in the peculiar manner of a sea that sustains no form of life. One would not exaggerate to say that the painter had made an experience possible for the percipient who afterwards chanced to look on his subject (and here one is inevitably reminded of issues raised in reference to Cézanne's approach to the landscapes which he painted). But the scene which Nash depicted was not a natural landscape; rather it was a monstrous *Gestalt* of human waste that he realised. His painting is of the nature of a comment, arguably the sort of comment that only the painter or the poet can achieve. Yet, if we say that he brings out the inwardness of the scene by enabling us so to see it, we realise that he does so not simply by eliciting the richness of what he views but rather by offering his vision as a supremely effective judgement on the civilisation whose fruits are there displayed before his eyes.

The example is significant in that it enables one again to do justice to the extent to which through the skill of poet, painter, dramatist, novelist, one may learn. Certainly, we all of us read for enjoyment, for entertainment, for relaxation; but (as we have seen) great novelists enlarge our understanding of the human world, awakening us to unnoticed depths, to its irregularities, sometimes bitter, sometimes comic, sometimes both at once, to the ways in which human lives in their concrete actuality defy the facile formulae of the moralist (unless he is wise enough to opt either for the extremes of formality in his exposition or for a use of concrete detail that on occasion may obscure from the uninitiated the general principles he would develop). But through painting of the sort I have used in my illustration, we are enabled to see what our senses reveal to us differently and that not in the sense in which we might claim to see it differently if we passed 'beyond the veil of perception'; yet not again as we might see it if (to quote the example of a cartoon I recall seeing in the *Daily Sketch* in boyhood) we followed the example of a fat little man who sharply terminates his wife's enjoyment of a sunset by remarking 'That reminds me; please remember that I like rather less streaky bacon than we have been having recently'! In the cartoon, the woman was soulful, the man crudely philistine and the cartoon was concerned to mark both alike. It is not that through Nash's work we are reminded by the sight of the dump of a dead sea as a man be reminded of hills he knows by the geometry of the clouds before him, or as men have been reminded of a crouching primeval beast by the sight of the exterior of King's College Chapel in Cambridge. To say that there is an analogy between dump and dead sea is to do no more than restate the problem. One may however quite properly insist that the use of the idiom of 'seeing as' in this example at least brings out the element of personal choice, the need at least of that amount of informed attention to allow the scene to reveal itself in the light of the painting.

Those who speak of faith as 'seeing as' certainly wish to emphasise the element of spontaneous commitment in the life of faith, extending from the initial decision to embark upon it (and of course this decision has its grounds) to the kind of awareness in which it issues. One has to ask whether the grounds on which the decision rests themselves include a preliminary 'seeing as' and if so whether this is the fruit of arbitrary decision, of a choice with as little foundation as a resolve to view the world as if it were engaged, unknown to itself, in a struggle with malign visitants from another planet, reaching towards us on flying saucers. Here, of course, we are immediately reminded of the story of Jesus and the suggestion is clear that in Christian faith we treat that tale as if it disclosed to us the ultimate order of the world. To do so is our own choice, elicited from us by meditation upon Jesus' history, the witness born to the mysterious sequel which allegedly followed his execution, etc. In treating this tale as a resolution, we do not act as Hegel did, when in his *Philosophy of Religion* he found in the theological presentation of the life of Jesus as movement from Galilee to Jerusalem, from life to death and thence to resurrection, a concrete realisation of the dialectical, self-reconciling order of the world. Rather, Jesus is received by those who use the tale of his life as a means of coming to see the world in a particular way as one who does not merely illustrate a principle but in some way (and here their exposition is often obscure) achieves it and brings it into being. The last addition is of course crucial and it is clear that a step has been taken from a way of seeing things to a pattern thrust upon human notice by the action of one through whom in history it is achieved. The step is crucial because it is a step from choice of viewpoint to assertion concerning that which is.

So too the metaphysician whose point of departure is of the sort suggested in this chapter proceeds in seeking to elaborate a view of the world that will enhance his understanding, even transform by rendering more subtle his perception, and enable him to guard his judgements against the crude unsophisticated acceptances of the morally philistine. It is thus that he finds himself compelled to attempt the utterance of the unutterable, representation of that which cannot be represented, even, moreover, to argue the claims of one form of representation against another as less inadequately conveying the shape of what is. If therefore in the following chapter we return to the problem of substance (treated earlier in this work with special reference to Aristotle) we do so because once we are engaged with the notion of substance, we are immediately aware that we are concerned with what is not a matter of our choice but what is thrust upon us.

14

Conclusion

Reference was made in preceding chapters to the depth of insight to be won from the poets. In returning to the treatment of the notion of substance, I would wish to begin by quoting three passages from a remarkable poem, 'On a Raised Beach' by Hugh MacDiarmid:

> Deep conviction or preference can seldom
> Find direct terms in which to express itself.
> To-day on this shingle shelf
> I understand this pensive reluctance so well,
> This not discommendable obstinacy,
> These contrivances of an inexpressive critical feeling,
> These stones with their resolve that Creation shall not be
> Injured by iconoclasts and quacks. Nothing has stirred
> Since I lay down this morning an eternity ago
> But one bird. The widest open door is the least liable to
>   intrusion,
> Ubiquitous as the sunlight, unfrequented as the sun.
> The inward gates of a bird are always open.
> It does not know how to shut them.
> That is the secret of its song,
> But whether any man's are ajar is doubtful.
> I look at these stones and know little about them,
> But I know their gates are open too,
> Always open, far longer open, than any bird's can be,
> That every one of them has had its gates wide open far
>   longer
> Than all birds put together, let alone humanity,
> Though through them no man can see,
> No man nor anything more recently born than themselves
> And that is everything else on the Earth.
> I too lying here have dismissed all else.
> Bread from stones is my sole and desperate dearth,

From stones, which are to the Earth as to the sunlight
Is the naked sun which is for no man's sight.
I would scorn to cry to any easier audience
Or, having cried, to lack patience to await the response.
I am no more indifferent or ill-disposed to life than death is;
I would fain accept it all completely as the soil does;
Already I feel all that can perish perishing in me
As so much has perished and all will yet perish in these
      stones.
I must begin with these stones as the world began.
Shall I come to a bird quicker than the world's course ran?
   To a bird, and to myself, a man?
   And what if I do, and further?
I shall only have gone a little way to go back again
And be alike a fleeting deceit of development,
Iconoclasts, quacks. So these stones have dismissed
All but all of evolution, unmoved by it,
(Is there anything to come they will not likewise dismiss?)
As the essential life of mankind in the mass
Is the same as their earliest ancestors yet.

Hot blood is of no use in dealing with eternity,
It is seldom that promises or even realisations
Can sustain a clear and searching gaze.
But an emotion chilled is an emotion controlled;
This is the road leading to certainty,
Reasoned planning for the time when reason can no longer
      avail.
It is essential to know the chill of all the objections
That come creeping into the mind, the battle between
      opposing ideas
Which gives the victory to the strongest and most universal
Over all others, and to wage it to the end
With increasing freedom, precision, and detachment
A detachment that shocks our instincts and ridicules our
      desires.

Men cannot hope
To survive the fall of the mountains
Which they will no more see than they saw their rise
Unless they are more concentrated and determined,
Truer to themselves and with more to be true to,

165

Than these stones, and as inerrable as they are.
Their sole concern is that what can be shaken
Shall be shaken and disappear
And only the unshakable be left.
What hardihood in any man has part or parcel in this
    latter?
It is necessary to make a stand and maintain it forever.
These stones go through Man, straight to God, if there
    is one.
What have they not gone through already?
Empires, civilisations, aeons.

At first sight, we seem in this poem a very long way from the
sort of issues that have concerned us in the discussion of Aristotle's
ontology. Again, both in the lines quoted and in the poem as a whole,
the mood is very different from that of the tentative essays on
theism, with which a considerable part of this work has been concerned. Yet the grave atheism expressed in the lines quoted effectively
latches on to the discontentment expressed in what has immediately
preceded it. The poet is concerned with what is; he is not inviting
the reader to an exercise in 'seeing as'. In some measure this is conveyed by the actual use in the poem of technical terms from geology,
of setting in the organisation of the whole the effective language
of the northern isles. It may sound paradoxical to say that the
philosopher who reads this poem may suddenly find himself reminded
of Kant's treatment of substance in the first *Analogy*, and this for a
number of reasons.

Firstly, Kant has been under fire for identifying the principle of
substantial permanence with the law of conservation of mass,
allegedly a flagrant example of his historical relativity. But,
however much he may have failed in supposing that he could
establish *a priori* a corrigible law, at least he recognises by his very
mistake an aspect of the complex problem of the interpenetration of
the metaphysical and the scientifically fundamental. A modern
student is concerned to disentangle; but what in Kant is woven
together is not without significance in the confused tapestry he
achieves in his relentless engagement with the problem of objectivity.

Secondly, it is indeed a poet's sense of substance as a very condition
of objectivity that MacDiarmid conveys. If the example of a poet,
Samuel Taylor Coleridge, shows us that a poet can learn from Kant

and by learning his own special lessons throw unexpected light on that philosopher's work, we are perhaps entitled to bring the work of poet and philosopher together in treating of this poem even as the poet has invoked a technical geological conceptual apparatus in his work. For Kant, the principle of substance is established particularly as the necessary condition of our awareness of time and the duration of time. One could say that Kant sometimes writes as if for him the rotation of the earth upon its axis about the sun could be regarded as a substance, because this regular cyclical process provides us with the means of reckoning the position of the days. Substance for Kant is a surrogate for time in general, enabling men to distinguish the rates at which things change and in the distinction of these rates, with the assistance of the parallel principle of causality, establish an indispensable for the very possibility of an objective world, actual, concrete instances of thinghood, understood as basic expressions of law. It is with the relation of law to objectivity that Kant in the *Analogies of Experience* is concerned. The world is not of our making; its fundamental orders do not express the haphazard play of our imaginings. Rather, that order is something in whose forms we may be confident in as much as without them there would be no objectivity; and one of these forms is the principle of substance.

Thirdly, MacDiarmid's objectivity is something more humanly poignant than Kant's rigorously defined and restricted concept. But it is an objectivity which meditation on the ancient rocks makes it possible for him to lay hold of; he is delivered from a self-regarding anthropocentrism, admitted to a serenely accepted atheism by finding in the relatively changeless rocky environment which he confronts an eloquent reminder of the relativity of human existence, of life itself. It is indeed an ontological relativity that he affirms. On the plane of being there is that which has been before human emergence upon the earth and will survive its disappearance.

The poet's language has a bite of which over-indulgent use across the centuries has deprived the idiom in which religious poets have spoken of divine eternity. Certainly, if God exists, then 'a thousand years in his sight are but as yesterday'. But Aristotle's first mover, whose activity is defined as *noēsis noēseōs* is too lightly dismissed by Christian theists as too coldly indifferent an ultimate to be bearable; this because to recall Aristotle's theology in the light of this poem is to be reminded that at least it honestly faced the question of what ultimately is, without prejudging the answer, that it must be an ultimate concerned with the human scene. MacDiarmid writes as an atheist and his poem is eloquent testimony that out of an atheist ontology a great poem may spring. To say this is not intended as the insult so often offered by the religious of claiming that no man is a serious atheist. But it is to remember that atheism and theism have this in common: that both alike are ontologies and that in the relatively loose sense of the term in which it may be applied to a conspectus of Aristotle's metaphysics that includes his theology as well as his anatomy of being. If it is insulting to the atheist to speak of him as unknown to himself a religious man, it is permissible to remember that unlike the positivist he allows himself to be concerned with what is, in the very special sense of demanding an unconditioned validity for what he says. Hence, indeed, the violence of Lenin's polemics against Bogdanov, for the latter's readiness to substitute Ernst Mach's sensationalism for materialism. No one would call Lenin's *Materialism and Empirio-Criticism* philosophy. It is polemic of the kind of which its formidable author is master. Yet it is the sort of work that the philosopher who is concerned with the problem of metaphysics would do well to remember and that not least in the present context as we recall the poetry that MacDiarmid has written in Lenin's honour.

In that man who may surely be regarded by his achievement as the greatest atheist of the twentieth century, there is no hint of a flabby humanism, or of the sort of intellectual indulgence which would suggest that we all intend the same provided only we can come to understand or accept one another. There are questions of ultimate truth and falsity; there are ontological questions, and if the Marxist is compelled to engage with the latter out of his social commitment, it must be with a kind of intellectual seriousness proportionate both to the questions themselves, the human context out of which they arise and the issues that turn upon their answer.

No contributor to the currently fashionable 'death of God' theology has engaged with Lenin. The present writer has often remarked that if he had a gift of pastiche, he would like nothing better than to essay a comment on the 'death of God' theology by the greatest atheist of the twentieth century and one of the greatest masters of ideological invective. The issues between theist and atheist are entirely serious, and if the former is all the time aware of the question thrust upon him by the positivist criticism of the very possibility of metaphysics, he should not forget what he has to learn also from the atheist. For if the atheist denies that God exists, he does so on the basis of his own apprenticeship in the school of the transcendent. He is almost obsessively preoccupied with what there is and with the implications of the objectivity of which MacDiarmid writes.

So we approach the definition of the problem of metaphysics with which this book has been concerned. It may have seemed that in the chapters immediately preceding the present we were moving towards a definition which would suggest that the metaphysician was concerned with the sorts of intimation men and women enjoyed of a transcendent order, intruding upon the world both natural and human in which they live. Yet it would be a grave mistake to oversimplify such a conception by suggesting that spiritual experience in the broadest sense was somehow self-justifying; or that we could argue somewhat after the manner of Descartes to a cause containing formally or eminently the ground of such experience. So here we recall again the sections of this book concerned with tragedy and the brief treatment of Christianity regarded as tragic in its essential teaching which was appended to them. What are we to say of this discussion in the light of that to which we have returned?

Koestler's experience in the jail at Malaga involved for him the purification of his own intentions for the future as the condition of his learning from it. But what did he learn? One could say that part of the lesson which he learned was that of the particularly tragic quality of the failure of the 1917 revolution and the tradition reshaped by its achievement and subsequent history which had helped both to make it possible and to receive new directions from it. His moral integrity demanded that he acknowledge the disappointment of these human hopes as something belonging to the stuff of things. Inevitably tragic perception rejects any method of dealing with the reality of evil by appeal to a facile teleology. It is the grossest insult to suffering men and women to suggest that their pain may provide a school in which others may learn lessons of self-knowledge and achieve a personal moral integrity. This is the fundamental 'lie in the soul' of much that is written by those who seek to make the so-called problem of evil disappear in the mists of a 'vale of soul making'. It is from the masters of the tragic experience that we learn to refuse to see things so. To this extent they are schoolmasters to issue some of the tough-minded into the seemingly hazardous world of transcendent ontology. One might even say that such a discipline is necessary if we are to avoid the sort of morass in which we will lose ourselves if we treat spiritual experience as self-justifying.

Yet again I shall be reminded of the emphasis laid in preceding chapters on just such experience; it is the point of departure. But to depart is not to arrive; rather it is simply to begin to engage. The questions with which we must engage are often conceptual; but more particularly they concern the hardly traceable relations of ontology, tragedy, poetry, religion. None may be swallowed up in the other and all alike are made aware that they stand in uneasy relation with the world of scientific description and explanation. So at the end of the enquiry we come to see that we have not resolved the problem of metaphysics, only at the level of a continued self-consciousness come to see aspects of it more clearly, come indeed dimly to perceive the sort of aliveness to connections which will refuse facile consolation but find in that refusal the suggestion that the issues are raised in the engagement. There is but little reference in this book to Pascal; but his name may come to the minds of some of those readers who have borne with the argument to this point. If I say that we have been reminded of the maxim 'simply connect', I should also say that we have also come to recognise the need for a restatement of Pascal's doctrine of the 'three orders' and of the kind of distinction and discontinuity he sought to affirm thereby. But the orders are different and the discontinuities are revealed in the statement of the problem.

Index of Proper Names

171